The Inspired Aquarium

QUARRY

The Inspired Aquarium

Ideas and Instructions for Living with Aquariums

GLOUCESTER MASSACHUSETTS

QUARRY BOOKS

Jeff Senske & Mike Senske

First published in the United States of America by
Quarry Books, a member of
Quayside Publishing Group
33 Commercial Street
Gloucester, Massachusetts 01930-5089
Telephone: (978) 282-9590
Fax: (978) 283-2742
www.rockpub.com

Library of Congress Cataloging-in-Publication Data
Senske, Jeff.
    The inspired aquarium : ideas and instructions for living with
aquariums / Jeff Senske
    and Mike Senske.
        p.   cm.
    ISBN 1-59253-195-4 (pbk.)
1. Aquariums. I. Senske, Mike. II. Title.
SF457.3.S46 2006
639.34—dc22   2006000776
                                              CIP

Printed in Singapore

ISBN 1-59253-195-4

10 9 8 7 6 5 4 3 2 1

Design: deep.co.uk
All photographs by Jeff Senske
Editor: Pat Price

Contents

Introduction

Aquariums are finding their way into our living spaces like never before—and with good reason. Replete with splendid fishes, exotic corals, and flourishing aquatic plants, an aquarium provides a soothing, welcome respite from our busy lives, while serving as both a beautiful design element and a distinctive conversation piece.

Thoughtfully composed and properly maintained, an aquarium breathes life into a room and provides a connection to nature within the home. It satisfies our innate fondness for proximity to water and offers movement, color, and light in a single fixture. Thanks to the strong trend toward making our homes the place in which we spend our leisure and entertainment time—consider the proliferation of cinema-quality home theaters and elaborate outdoor areas, for example—custom aquarium installations are soaring in popularity, and homeowners and designers are integrating aquariums into their spaces. Major advancements in aquarium technology, construction, and custom installation techniques, combined with a more expansive knowledge of long-term care and maintenance, have made exceptional aquarium installations more accessible than ever.

Before committing to a new aquarium, however, you should arm yourself with all the necessary information. This book provides core knowledge for anyone with the desire to bring nature into the home through the magic of an aquarium. We will explore issues for newcomers and novices, and provide visual inspiration and useful tips for advanced hobbyists. Sections on freshwater and saltwater aquariums provide an understanding of the differences—both practical and visual—between the different aquarium styles, so you can make an informed decision in determining the type of aquarium style that's right for your space, time, and budget. The sections also include suggestions for fish, plants, and corals, without confusing you with technical jargon and scientific names.

Whether you are considering your first aquarium or want to improve your layout skills, plan a custom installation, or improve an existing system you care for yourself, the ideas and concepts in this book will help you achieve an inspired aquarium.

←

A 200-gallon (757-liter) live-planted aquarium breathes life into this spacious home. The aquarium can be enjoyed from many points in the space, thanks to careful planning during the design phase.

→

Even a small aquarium can positively affect a room. This 72-gallon (272-liter) bowfront aquarium is a standard production model, right off the showroom floor. The bowed glass front panel makes for a decorative presence, and both the aquascape and lighting choice emphasize the aquarium as an effective design focal point in this urban loft.

Part 01: Placement and Planning

The modern aquarium has come of age, and when approached as a design element or focal point—as living sculpture and not just a fish tank—it is an impressive addition to any interior. The question is: Where do you begin? What originates as a thing of beauty can quickly become an eyesore if it is not properly planned and managed from the start. Placement, cabinetry and millwork, lighting—both functional and aesthetic—filtration and life support, saltwater or freshwater style, decorative elements, and layout composition (the aquascape), plus maintenance and long-term care are important issues to consider when planning an aquarium installation.

Arming yourself with a knowledge of basic aquarium keeping and general terminology helps you better understand any aquarium system. This is an asset when hiring a professional company to install your aquarium, because it allows you to effectively communicate your needs regarding noise, heat, and options such as converting from one type of installation to another in the future. Should you plan to install the aquarium yourself, having a good grasp of filtration, lighting, temperature control, and other maintenance basics will help you navigate the dizzying number of choices available.

↖ ↑

Different spaces, different needs. Each of these aquariums plays a
different role in the room. One complements a simple, contemporary
space; the other was designed for a room that is more ornate and
traditional. Aquarium style, cabinetry, and the aquascape were clearly
considered early in the design process for each. The results are
aquariums that match the respective aesthetic philosophies of
the homeowners.

Chapter 1:
Where to Place Your Aquarium

The decision to incorporate an aquarium into the home is easy enough to make—at least from the standpoint of sheer desire to have one. While the modern aquarium and accompanying equipment have come a long way toward making successful aquarium-keeping a reality, one must still become familiar with quite a body of knowledge to ensure success. The process begins with the most fundamental question: Where do I put my aquarium? In many spaces, the answer is obvious; in others, it may require a little creative vision, perhaps from an aquarium installation consultant (usually available through local installation and maintenance companies; see Resources, page 170), interior designer, or architect. Throughout the planning phase, imagine various angles of view, possible dimensions, desired impact on the space, and, of course, the types of fish and aquatic life you'd like to include.

Impact on the Space

Probably your first consideration when deciding where to place your aquarium is determining its impact on the space. If you want your aquarium to be a focal point, requiring a prominent place in the room, an island aquarium—one that can be viewed from all sides—or an open-ended room divider might be the answer. If you prefer that the aquarium play a complementary role—a simple point of interest in the room rather than its focus—consider placing it in an interesting nook or incorporating it into existing millwork or cabinetry.

Freestanding corner installations offer a distinctive alternative to traditional placements and provide interesting opportunities for the aquascape due to their depth and unusual triangular proportions. Even small aquariums of less than 50 gallons (189 liters) can provide atmosphere, especially in lofts or small rooms and on desks or tabletops.

←

A simple live-planted aquarium subtly adorns this conversation area. Thoughtful placement creates an effectual interplay between the two arched windows and the aquarium. The green of the plants and other natural tones pair well with the wood trim and other interior features.

→

The bright and bold nature of this island/room-divider installation makes a strong impact on the space, and is visible from many points, including the dining area and kitchen. Bowed glass adds depth and character.

→

The impact of the other side of the aquarium installation is decidedly variable, placing less demand on the viewer's attention. The aquarium is not the focal point here. Instead, it provides an effective diversion from watching television or reading.

Support Structure

Even if you know exactly where you want to place the aquarium, you must determine the position from which you will view it: seated, standing, or in between. This greatly affects the support stand height and may, in the end, cause you to rethink an initial placement idea. The average height of a production aquarium stand (those available from a local fish or pet store) is 32 inches (81 cm). Although this height works well for smaller aquariums of fewer than 100 gallons (380 liters) or in a small room, most custom-made aquariums begin at 42 inches (107 cm). At this height, the aquarium is not too low to be viewed while standing and not too high to be viewed while seated. The best height for your space, however, might well be higher or lower than 42 inches (107 cm).

Note that many aquarium manufacturers require, for warranty purposes, that the aquarium be placed on their support stand. Even a custom-made aquarium with custom cabinetry or millwork on or around the stand requires a raw support structure supplied by the aquarium manufacturer. This ensures that the support is placed correctly.

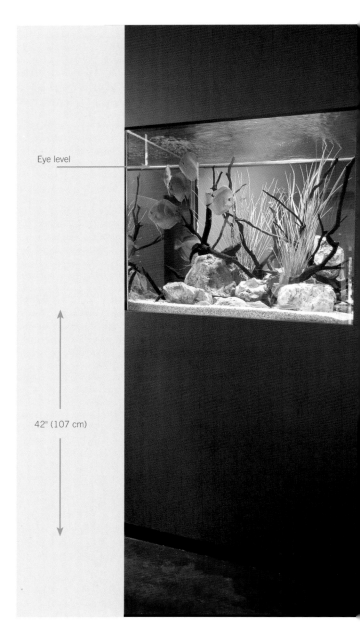

Eye level

42" (107 cm)

↑
This aquarium support stand, at 42 inches (107 cm), is designed for optimal viewing from a standing position. Eye-level interaction with an aquarium is a desirable feature in areas such as foyers, in which people rarely sit for any length of time.

Design Tip

Take the time to picture the placement of the aquarium from various positions in the room, and keep a tape measure handy to approximate ideal heights for the support structure. Don't forget to include the desired height of the glass box itself when envisioning the finished aquarium.

Making It Easy:
Proximity to Drain and Fill

If possible, place your aquarium within reach of a drain and replacement water source. This is more easily accomplished with new construction, when it is possible to incorporate built-in drains and water outlets either right under or near the support stand. Of course, you can add these fixtures to existing settings as part of a remodel, but making accommodations for them in the design and building stage is much easier and should be considered in new construction situations.

Drain and fill spaces can include dedicated closets or areas behind the tank with sinks and drains, in which water purification equipment, hoses, and supplies can be kept. Simply having a

dedicated drain and faucet under the tank makes water changes much faster and easier than if the water source is at a distance. Often, the drain valve can be incorporated into the bottom of the aquarium via a bulkhead fitting. A length of hose or plumbing runs straight to the drain, and opening a valve starts the water change. For freshwater aquariums, a simple hose-fitting faucet nearby or under the tank can provide fill water on demand. Attaching a small filter bottle filled with activated carbon in line from the faucet removes the chlorine from municipal tap water supplies—in most instances, all the treatment tap water needs. Keep in mind that the average water change on a freshwater aquarium is about 50 percent of the tank volume.

↓

A straightforward drain hole and faucet are directly under the aquarium, inside the cabinetry. A short length of siphon hose runs from the tank to the drain (a). The faucet provides a water source right at hand for easy refilling (b).

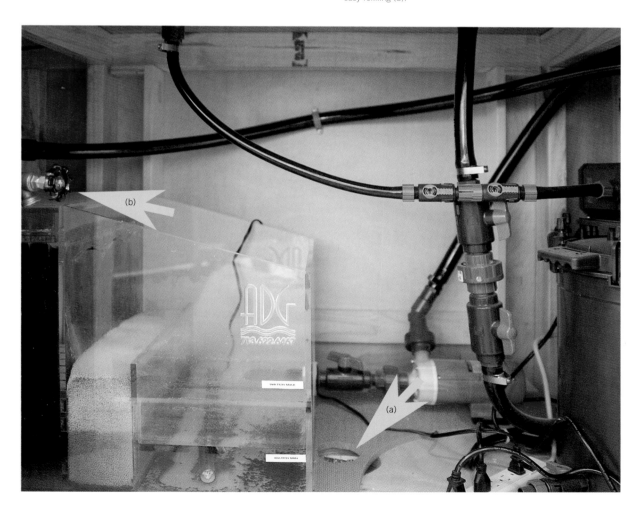

If you cannot arrange for a nearby sink or drain, you can use hoses to reach a faucet and to siphon drain water into the nearest toilet (a properly functioning toilet automatically flushes when filled, so you do not need to worry about it overflowing). But without question, having these fixtures at hand makes the routine maintenance much easier. And when it comes to long-term care, ease is the name of the game!

Both drain setups can also apply to some saltwater aquariums. However, the source water for a saltwater aquarium requires more preparation because salt and other components must be added before the water goes into the aquarium. Also, because municipal tap water supplies are unsuitable for saltwater aquariums, extensive purification is necessary.

Here again, forethought and planning in the system design can go a long way toward making long-term maintenance much easier (and less expensive!). Many aquarium maintenance companies offer a lower service charge per visit when the source water is near the aquarium or when on-site mixing of the replacement water is available. A common approach is to install a sufficiently large vat or plastic water tank with a circulation pump either in a dedicated area behind the tank, where the installation permits, or in a garage or storage area. The vat is filled with purified water from a reverse osmosis or deionization unit, and salt is then added by hand. The result is a ready-to-use source of fresh, properly dissolved saltwater.

Design Tip
Consider having a custom aquarium made with holes drilled through the bottom for filter inflows and outflows. The filters, plus unsightly hoses and tubing, can be easily concealed by the aquascape.

Room to Breathe:
Special Ventilation Considerations

When considering the location of your aquarium, you must also think about allowing space for ventilation. Adequate ventilation for lighting and specialized equipment is paramount to ensuring the long-term health of your aquarium's inhabitants, particularly saltwater aquariums.

Unlike most tropical freshwater species, most saltwater fish and invertebrates commonly collected for aquariums require a water temperature slightly lower than the average room temperature, ideally between 74° and 78°F (23° and 26°C).

Even if the average room temperature falls into this range, keeping the water at a constant ideal temperature actually requires a much colder room temperature due to the heat generated by the aquarium's high-powered lighting (see below). Consistent water temperature is extremely important for aquarium inhabitants; temperature fluctuations weaken their immune systems and can make them prone to disease. For this reason, a chiller (rather than a heater, which is used to maintain temperatures in freshwater aquariums) has become the standard and, in most expert opinions, required equipment on modern saltwater installations. Essentially a small refrigeration unit, a chiller cools the aquarium water and keeps it at a constant cool temperature.

← The chiller on this saltwater system is vented by a fan positioned directly beneath it (far left).

← The air is able to escape through the bottom of the support stand, which is raised to accommodate this need (left).

↑ Here, a hole was cut to fit a small fan that vents heat produced within the fully enclosed cabinetry by the aquarium lighting.

↓ Air comes out through a traditional vent. When necessary, vents like this can be painted to be less conspicuous.

However, just like your refrigerator, these units give off heat that must be removed or vented, or the unit will break down. For this reason, you must be sure that the space you have in mind for a saltwater aquarium can accommodate the chiller as well as a suitable ventilation method. This can be a simple inflow/outflow vent setup with one or two fans pulling or pushing the heated air out. An option is to place the chiller outdoors or in a garage or storage area that can be easily ventilated.

Lighting also generates heat. Saltwater reef aquariums use intense, high-wattage light fixtures to stimulate and grow live corals, while powerful lighting is used in freshwater live-planted aquariums to encourage photosynthesis and plant growth. These fixtures can produce enough heat to affect water temperature. While adding a chiller to a freshwater live-planted aquarium would be overkill, the plants in these habitats prefer slightly cooler temperatures (see chapter 6).

Good ventilation of the lighting area is the key to temperature consistency, and it allows chillers to operate efficiently. In addition, if the chiller fails some time before you notice, a properly ventilated lighting area will contribute less to rising water temperature. Simple fans and vents usually suffice.

Ventilation is not an issue with most basic decorative freshwater aquariums (those without live plants). The fish typically prefer slightly warmer water, and tank heaters and incidental warmth from lighting are beneficial, although too much temperature fluctuation caused by light fixtures should be avoided. The key is to be sure that the space you are thinking about for the aquarium can accommodate special needs.

The Noise Factor

Because saltwater aquariums require more equipment, they are generally noisier than freshwater systems. (Most freshwater aquariums are fine with just simple canister filters, which are virtually silent.) The recirculation pump used to return water from the equipment underneath (or otherwise outside the aquarium) to the tank is often the main culprit, but the more plumbing and devices involved, the greater the opportunity for unwanted noise. Tile and hardwood flooring can also amplify the vibrations of the pumps and equipment.

If a saltwater tank is in your plans, consider the extent to which potential noise issues, such as the continuous hum of a magnet drive pump or the on cycle of a chiller unit, will affect you. Although you can reduce noise through insulation and high-tech sound dampening, some low-level noise generally remains.

The overflow box, which is standard on saltwater systems to get water from the aquarium down to the sump, and additional equipment, such as chillers and protein skimmers, can also be a source of water noise. Fortunately, great strides have been made in devising ways to minimize the sound the water makes as it spills over and flows down the overflow box to the plumbing— a sound some find relaxing and others find annoying.

Areas to Avoid

When considering placement, a few locations should either be ruled out right away or at least given careful consideration, even if they seem perfect at first. Proximity to windows, for example, can be problematic. A primary issue is excessive glare, which detracts from enjoyment of the aquascape. Often not considered when envisioning placement, high or varying degrees of glare can spoil daytime viewing. Direct sunlight through the windows can also cause problems with heat and algae growth, while cool air near windows in winter can contribute to temperature fluctuations.

High traffic areas should also be avoided. Excessive human traffic can cause shy fish to hide or be easily frightened. It is not uncommon for fish to wound themselves on rocks or other hard decorative elements as they seek cover from loud noises, such as slamming doors and other recurring shocks or vibrations. While some fish grow accustomed to the traffic, many experience ongoing stress and either hide all the time or even perish. Delicate saltwater fish are particularly sensitive to noise and traffic, as are timid, peaceful-natured freshwater ornamentals.

→

This filtration system runs a live coral reef aquarium installed in a home theater. Because pump or water noise was a major concern, the equipment was placed outside.

↓

The large pump and chiller powering this large reef aquarium generate a lot of noise. Here, simple indoor/outdoor carpet was used to dampen excess noise, while also lending a nicer look to the cabinetry interior. This installation also features sound dampening foam padding on the bottom of the cabinetry interior, which greatly reduces vibration noise from the main pump.

Chapter 2:
Choosing an Aquarium

Once you have decided where to place your aquarium, your next move is to choose the one that's right for you. Aquarium construction and dimensions, maintenance access, installation style (freestanding, built-in, island, etc.), and cabinetry all influence the effect, long-term function, and enjoyment of the final product. Remember that with many installation styles, the aquarium is an integrated fixture that can be quite costly to rip out or modify once in place. It pays, therefore, to spend time determining the objectives of the aquarium in the space, and how best to balance those objectives with maintenance and other compulsory aspects of aquarium ownership.

Size Matters:
Considering a Larger Aquarium

Initial maintenance concerns aside, when it comes to aquariums, as a general rule, bigger is better. The larger the water volume, the less fluctuation of any given parameter will occur over time; maintaining consistency is generally easier in a larger aquarium. Bear in mind, however, that this equation begins to shift against ease of maintenance at some point. Consider going with the largest tank possible for the given area, up to about 1,000 gallons (3,784 liters). When aquariums are larger than this, the dynamics of installation, equipment, and maintenance begin to change.

The average residential aquarium installation is 150 to 500 gallons (568 to 1,892 liters); within this range, equipment and requirements vary little. Enormous potential for high-impact aquascapes exists in this size range, and most aquarium service companies are well equipped to manage them. If you plan to do your own maintenance, an aquarium in this range is realistic and helps minimize the potential for spending more time maintaining the aquarium than enjoying it.

Don't Get too High: The Importance of Proportion

Perhaps the most important dimension to consider is height. There is a natural tendency to want a large viewing window; people want to stand before a massive wall of water like those in public aquariums and zoo exhibits. While it can be striking, an excessively tall aquarium brings with it potential challenges, particularly when designed for a residential space.

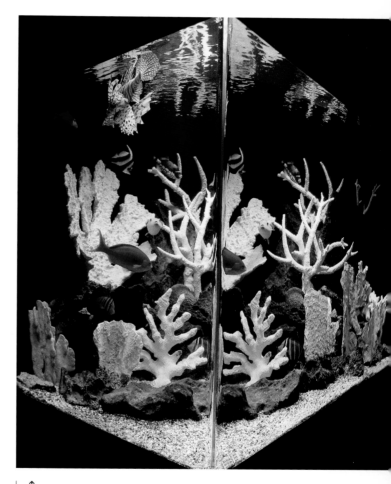

↑
At 48 inches (122 cm) tall, this installation represents the upper range of practical aquarium height. A taller aquarium is certainly possible, but access and ease-of-maintenance variables (such as the ability to reach the bottom without climbing in) can become real problems.

←
A custom-made concave aquarium curves perfectly with the wall. The classic built-in design with marble-trim enclosure makes an elegant design statement.

Foremost among these challenges is accessibility. Few maintenance professionals and even fewer aquarium hobbyists are able to physically get inside a tall aquarium for maintenance, so depths beyond the average reach of a person's arm can pose problems. Tall aquariums can be difficult to maintain—when a decorative element falls over or must be adjusted, for example—and limiting, in terms of the aquarium layout or composition, because compositional elements that reach the top of the volume are hard to come by. This is especially true when working with live-planted aquariums or reef aquariums in which all the interior components of the aquarium are natural. Very large rocks, for example, are often too heavy to get into the tank. Once they are installed, manipulating them can be even more difficult. Although man-made corals and fabricated inserts can be used if a tall tank is desired, access and reach are still at issue.

The easier an aquarium is to access and maintain, the more it will receive the maintenance it requires, whether by you or a maintenance professional. For this reason, think in terms of maximizing size and impact through length and width rather than height. The balance will pay off in the long run.

The current standard for maximum height for a glass aquarium is approximately 42 inches (107 cm). While a few custom fabricators are willing to make taller glass aquariums, their cost is typically much higher and their overall structural integrity and long-term strength may be compromised. The average maximum length is 10 feet (3 m), though again, some manufacturers may be willing to make them larger.

Acrylic aquariums can be made to virtually any height, but, as stated before, greater heights can lead to composition and maintenance problems. Length and width are of little concern with acrylic, which makes it the preferred material for large-scale installations.

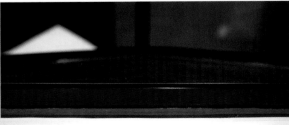

The Great Debate: Glass versus Acrylic

Many have debated the virtues of one over the other for aquarium construction. Most of us are familiar with the glass aquariums available at the local pet shop and have probably seen acrylic aquariums or viewing panels in public aquariums. Shark displays and multi-thousand-gallon exhibits in which scuba divers handfeed the inhabitants come to mind. Both glass and acrylic have their strong points, and either can be used for most residential installations.

Acrylic aquariums have a reputation for scratching more easily than glass, and some early polymers were known to yellow over time. To some, acrylic also has a noticeably plastic appearance. It is, however, exceedingly strong because its edges are chemically bonded, rather than glued together, as are glass aquariums. This gives acrylic a substantial edge in terms of leak protection; the chemical bond is actually stronger than the acrylic panels it holds together.

Acrylic can also be molded into a wide variety of shapes. Curves and bends, both concave and convex, are easily achieved due to the greater flexibility of the material. Abstract shapes are also possible with acrylic. For tanks exceeding 10 feet (3 m) in length or 45 inches (114 cm) in height, acrylic is the only choice.

Glass aquariums are less prone to scratching, although they will scratch if care is not taken when executing a new layout or performing maintenance. High-quality glass aquariums generally project a more refined appearance, and can seem more elegant, than acrylic aquariums of equal dimensions. Construction techniques have advanced significantly; now bold bowfront designs and even canoe or double bowfront aquariums are available for applications where the aquarium is viewed from two or more sides. Super-high-clarity glass that shows no green or blue tinting is also available. Known as low-iron glass, this ultra-clear variety can cost twice as much as regular glass, but it offers noticeably higher clarity.

←

Design and engineering improvements in the construction of custom-made aquariums have helped make them stronger and more leak-resistant than ever. This cross-section, provided by Oceanic Systems, Inc., shows the layering of materials and steel-reinforced outer support designed to keep the aquarium intact, even if the bottom glass fails.

Aquarium Designs

A wealth of installation styles, from traditional freestanding aquariums to innovative designs that harmonize the aquarium with the surrounding space, are available to make your in-home aquatic dreams a reality.

Choosing the right design for you can be difficult, however, particularly in new construction situations where the possibilities are open-ended. As is true of most major design decisions, the sooner the aquarium is incorporated into the plans or blueprints, the more likely it is that accommodations can be made and the installation comes off as flawlessly as possible. In other words, you cannot plan soon enough for the aquarium! But even if your decision to include an aquarium comes late in construction or is part of a remodel, with the right information, forethought, and planning, aquariums can still be seamlessly integrated into the space.

Design Tip
Installing a galvanized drip pan underneath the aquarium greatly diminishes the impact of leaks or drips from the aquarium or system plumbing (hoses, unions, valves, filter disconnects, etc.). When the pan is coupled with a built-in floor drain underneath the aquarium, the likelihood of floor damage from incidental leaks is very low.

↑

The difference between regular glass (left) and low-iron glass (right) is clear. But is it worth the extra cost? That depends on both taste and budget.

Classic Design: Freestanding Aquariums

Almost everyone is familiar with the freestanding aquarium-and-stand combination: the simple wrought-iron stand supporting a thick, black-rimmed tank, or a bulky pine cabinet stand with faux wood trim. Rest assured, those days are gone—the modern freestanding aquarium can be customized to fit into any décor, with wood materials, laminates, and even metallic finishes available. Any finish designed for cabinetry can be applied to the aquarium. Most custom freestanding options include matching canopy tops, a tasteful and complementary way to conceal the light fixtures on the tank.

Freestanding aquariums can be placed just about anywhere and are by far the most versatile in the long term because they can be moved with far greater ease than built-in options. Standard-issue production aquariums, such as those available in local fish or pet shops, have enjoyed some design improvements over the years. Popular wood trims, such as pine, cherry, oak, and walnut, are available, as are progressive options that incorporate wood and stainless steel, glass doors, and combinations of woods. Matching canopies are usually standard. It is possible to enliven a room simply and affordably by choosing the right production aquarium system.

The Fourth Dimension: Open-Top Tanks

Imagine an aquascape in which dramatic and sculptural pieces of driftwood break the water's surface or in which aquatic plants grow freely and flower above the waterline. Imagine viewing the inhabitants not just from the front and sides of the aquarium, as is typical, but from above, which reveals an altogether different perspective. Within the freestanding aquarium category is another interesting and innovative design: the open-top aquarium. Here, the aquascape designer uses the space above the waterline to create dramatic effects and add another dimension to aquarium viewing.

Open-top aquariums are versatile in terms of placement in the space, but they do pose lighting challenges because the fixtures and associated hardware generally must be suspended from the ceiling. Solutions are available, however; Aqua Design Amano, a Japanese manufacturer, offers a suspension system that attaches to the aquarium stand, and similar fixture designs are in the works. Sleek and sophisticated, these fixtures are often among the most thoughtfully designed, due in part to their placement in plain view. (See chapter 6 for more examples of open-top aquariums.)

↑
Modern production aquariums and stands have vastly improved. This freestanding model incorporates stainless steel laminates and an upgraded smoked-glass door for a clean, sophisticated look.

↑
The open-top style is often used for live-planted aquariums so that the plants can grow out of the top. Here, a few species are just starting to break the water's surface.

Island Style: Aquariums Viewed from All Sides

One of the most interesting types of freestanding aquarium is the island-style installation. A real architectural focal point, an island-style aquarium provides an underwater panorama visible from all sides and angles. It can serve many functions within the space: to break up monotony, divide open areas, or just look beautiful on its own.

Island installations can require more planning than other aquarium styles, mostly to route the electricity either down from the ceiling or up from the floor. Either way, the power cords can run from bottom to top or top to bottom via one of two common methods. One is to route all the cords through the overflow box that provides passage of the aquarium water to the filtration or sump in the cabinet below. An additional hole is drilled in the aquarium bottom and a completely dry route is created (usually with PVC tubing) in which the power cords are safely bundled. This option is effective for getting power or extension cords to the top or bottom of the aquarium regardless of whether the power source is above or below the installation.

The other method is to route only necessary power cords through a chase or edge covering mounted on a corner of the aquarium. Usually a chase is added to all four corners for consistency of appearance.

Beyond the special needs of routing power, the next most significant aspect to consider is the aquascape for the island aquarium. Careful attention must be paid to the placement of the compositional elements to ensure a balanced and pleasing look from all sides and angles. This can prove challenging, so be prepared to spend significant time laying out the aquarium, or be sure the aquascape designer has experience (or confidence, whichever comes first!) with island compositions.

Some design forethought may be required to devise the best choice for the aquarium top. Traditional canopy tops are fine, but two people may be needed to remove them due to the island aquarium's greater bulk. A better idea is to use fixed access doors, which allow easy access for maintenance and eliminate the need for a cumbersome canopy.

Design Tip

Choosing Custom over Production
For any installation that requires custom cabinetry, millwork, or framing, especially on built-in aquariums, choose a custom-made aquarium over a production or mass-produced option. Most production aquariums have plastic or wood-grained trim around the top and bottom perimeters that prevents the tank from sitting flush against the framing wall, leaving unsightly gaps.

↑
An impressive installation becomes the focal point of what is often the most popular space in the home—the kitchen. A seating area gives this aquarium functionality, while the island-style placement provides a wealth of viewing potential.

↑
This side view reveals the added dimension of an island installation.

Backgrounds

One of the most common options for aquariums positioned against a wall or with sides or panels that need concealing is to paint the glass black. Black adds depth and eliminates the view of wires or tubing that may be routed behind the aquarium. It is a neutral color against which most decorative elements show nicely.

A simple roller application of an oil-based flat black paint—on the outside, of course—gives the fastest and easiest coverage, and the paint can be scraped off should you decide to do something different in the future. Shades of blue can also be used.

Avoid traditional taped-on backgrounds; these tend to bend and wrinkle over time, and any water that splashes or drips between the background and the glass shows through the aquarium. Not only are these water spots unsightly, but the mineral deposits left behind after the water evaporates can be difficult and sometimes impossible to remove.

Tinting films that adhere to the aquarium are also available; however, care must be taken to not get them wet.

Variation on a Theme: The Peninsula Aquarium

Ideal for creating a partial divide between areas, the peninsula aquarium comes off a single wall and adds a third angle of view at one end, lending itself to unusual layout opportunities. As with any multisided aquarium, the aquascape should take advantage of these multiple angles so the aquarium maintains an attractive presence from the several points from which it is seen. All tubes, hoses, and wires can be routed on or toward the wall end for easy consolidation and concealment.

Best of Both Worlds: The Freestanding Room Divider

At first glance, it is easy to assume that this installation style is built into the wall. Nicely framed on one side while supported on the other by a freestanding cabinet and matching canopy top, the freestanding room divider offers two distinct advantages: the ease and convenience of placing the aquarium on a custom support structure—with all of the options for harmonizing the cabinetry to the space—plus the impact and appeal of what appears to be a built-in installation. Framed and seamless, the aquarium appears as a liquid canvas: fine living art on your wall.

This installation style allows many variations. In fact, the room-divider aquarium is an option in almost any space with a dividing wall that can support the cut-out for the framed side and has sufficient space on the opposite side of the wall to position the support stand. Cabinetry or millwork around the aquarium on the support side provides greater versatility and an integrated appearance.

Design Tip

Multisided Installation Aquascapes

For multisided installations, be sure to plan an aquascape that takes into account the two sides of the viewing perspective so elements of both sides complement the finished look. An effective technique is to include open ends in the composition so fish may easily make their way around the layout.

Additional Views

When sizing up an area for a room-divider aquarium or built-in, look for opportunities to create additional viewing windows or reveals. These add visual interest and help the aquarium interact with the space. For example, create a third view on one end of a built-in aquarium to reveal the aquascape to people passing in a hall or walkway who otherwise would see just a wall or the end of the aquarium cabinetry. This additional view can be almost like adding a second aquarium to the space.

→

This peninsula-style installation extends the aquarium into the surrounding space and affects viewing from a seating area (a), the kitchen (b), and the entryway (c).

←

Perfectly framed on the kitchen side, this decorative saltwater aquarium has a well-planned, built-in look. Note that the aquascape design was kept open to allow views between the divided spaces.

←

A beautiful example of a freestanding room-divider aquarium with a lovely one-piece custom cabinetry support stand and top enclosure on the living room side.

(a)

(b)

(c)

The Classic Built-In Aquarium

When most people hear the term custom aquarium, they think of the classic built-into-the-wall installation. With its clean lines and integrated appearance, the built-in satisfies the desire for an aquarium that is truly part of the home.

The primary consideration is access to the aquarium, which depends on the desired finished appearance of the front. Access can be through doors above the aquarium; these can be propped up, opened like regular cabinet doors, or supported by hinges. Removable panels are another option, but these are probably best for aquariums limited to approximately 6 feet (2 m) long,

so they can be easily removed by one person. When possible, back access is preferred, as it provides greater opportunity for thorough maintenance. Space permitting, back access areas can also be used for storage, water purification filters, or equipment needed for saltwater systems.

Installing a built-in aquarium as part of a new construction offers few constraints outside of budget. However, if the aquarium is part of a remodel or installation in an existing space, be sure the wall in which you want to place it is not load-bearing or otherwise crucial to the stability of the structure. Consult an engineer or your contractor/builder for assistance in determining if a particular wall is load-bearing or not.

A Word on Cabinetry

Regardless of the installation style you choose, chances are that some form of custom cabinetry will be necessary. You can probably find plenty of talented and highly skilled cabinet and millwork professionals who are capable of handling the basic requirements for aquarium cabinetry. However, most are likely to have limited experience with it and may not realize the importance of the many details that can make or break the final product. Even a minor annoyance can diminish your enjoyment of an otherwise beautiful installation. Here are useful tips to convey to the professional handling your aquarium framing or custom cabinetry.

↑
Contemporary aquarium cabinetry can incorporate materials other than wood and plastic laminates. This live coral reef aquarium is given a high-tech feel by means of the textured stainless-steel laminate material over the wood core.

↙
A classic built-in aquarium with a twist! Instead of the usual painting hung over a bed, these homeowners chose a true work of living art for their bedroom. Access is from behind, via one of the master closets.

↓
The full installation on the second floor.

↘
A freestanding aquarium on the second floor is visible from the first-floor foyer and stairwell through a well-planned cut out.

Design Tip

Chiller Placement
Chillers for saltwater installations can be placed outside the aquarium stand. With a bit of simple plumbing, chillers can be easily installed in garages, dedicated closet areas, or even outside (except in harsh climates). Some protection from the elements is typically all that is required for outdoor installations. The key is to ensure that the unit can breathe.

Top and Bottom Clearances

One of the most common oversights when building aquarium cabinetry involves the amount of reveal at the waterline. Regardless of the installation type—removable canopy or built-in—the finish around the top of the aquarium should come down far enough so the waterline is not visible. This is important for two reasons. First, as evaporation occurs, the waterline drops. Properly built cabinetry or framing can delay the unsightly appearance of a low waterline. Second, although many aquariums are equipped with automatic top-off systems or filters that keep the water level in the aquarium constant, too much of the top or bottom of the aquarium showing is simply unattractive. Covering a minimum of 1½ to 2 inches (4 to 5 cm) at the top solves this problem. Covering about the same amount of the tank bottom is also good practice. The glass thickness of the base determines exactly how much should be concealed, but a good strategy is to cover up to about the first inch (1.5 cm) of the bottom with gravel or substrate, if only to maintain consistency of the framing at both top and bottom.

Minimizing or Eliminating Light Escape

A common problem that can be easily addressed in the planning and design phase is light leakage through cracks between millwork panels, framing, or—most commonly—through front access doors that are opened regularly for feeding.

While this problem can be remedied by inserting a small black cover piece over the cracks, being aware of potential problems beforehand allows for design modifications early on and reduces the need for follow-up tweaks and callbacks to the builder.

Ventilation

As noted in chapter 1, some installations, especially saltwater, require ventilation to accommodate chillers or high-wattage light fixtures. Design forethought for the cabinetry in this regard is paramount. You do not want to discover that the system is not sufficiently ventilated after the aquarium is already stocked and running!

The beautiful and popular coral reef aquarium is perhaps the biggest potential victim of ventilation problems because the average system requires a significant amount of heat-producing equipment. Also, although most aquarium inhabitants are subject to health and disease threats in a fluctuating environment, corals and other invertebrates are particularly sensitive to temperature shifts.

It is much easier to introduce adequate ventilation at the beginning of a project. Each system and installation is different, so needs vary, but integrated fans and vents require special consideration when it comes to cabinetry. Coordination between the homeowner/project manager, the aquarium professional, and the cabinetmaker is essential.

←
Faux finishing and ornate cast iron detailing give this freestanding freshwater aquarium distinctive class and character. Elsewhere in the space, the coffee table and chandelier feature similar iron shapes.

→
These canopies were made without access doors on the front or sides to maintain a clean look, so a simple feeding door was cut into the canopy top for access. The feeding doors are not visible when viewing the aquarium.

Design Tip

Matching Cabinetry
A good cabinetmaker can match aquarium cabinetry to existing cabinetry throughout the home or near the aquarium. This goes far in integrating the aquarium with the home.

Feeding Holes
Be sure to incorporate these into aquarium tops and canopies for an easy way to feed the fish. Feeding doors or holes should be easily accessible. Where possible, create a design that allows feeding at various points in the aquarium. This is especially useful in larger aquariums. It also keeps the fish from becoming conditioned to hover near the same spot for food.

Chapter 3:
Filtration

The filtration system is the heart of the aquarium. Proper filtration is vital to creating a successful aquarium, yet many people compromise on the filtration system in favor of fancy cabinetry or more exotic fish. Don't make this mistake! A balanced filtration system includes all the filter types necessary to maintain consistent water quality so when it's time to splurge on those exotic fish, conditions are right to support them. This chapter details all aspects of aquarium filtration. (Specific filtration applications for freshwater and saltwater styles are found in their respective chapters).

A Polished Performance: Mechanical Filtration

Removing particulate matter from the water efficiently and consistently is the best defense against a cloudy or dirty-looking aquarium. Mechanical filtration uses filters or absorbent filter materials such as special sponges, bonded filter pads, and filter floss to physically trap and remove particulate matter from the aquarium water. These materials are placed in areas of constant water flow such as a canister filter or trickle-filter overflow box or sump, all of which are discussed later in this chapter. Mechanical filter material requires the most consistent routine cleaning because of the continuous accumulation of tiny debris particles in the media. Cleaning involves either rinsing or replacing the material.

←

For freshwater aquariums, more than one type of filtration can be used to boost water quality, maintain superior clarity, and enable the keeping of numerous kinds of fish. This decorative freshwater aquarium uses both trickle and canister filtration.

The Battle for Purity: Chemical Filtration

Chemical filtration methods and media are often incorporated into mechanical and biological types of filtration (see below). These include products such as activated carbon or charcoal, which are highly porous and can absorb large amounts of unwanted gases and other potential toxins from aquarium water, significantly increasing purity. Chemical filter media can also eliminate most water discoloration. For example, many varieties of decorative driftwood used in freshwater tanks cause the water to yellow when it is first placed in the aquarium. Chemical filtration, along with initial frequent partial water changes, can greatly reduce the amount of time required to permanently clear the water.

Many function-specific types of chemical filtration are available for saltwater and saltwater reef aquariums. Most are designed to absorb metabolic byproducts or are otherwise specially formulated to help create an oceanlike environment.

↑
Bonded filter pads and foam sponges are common types of mechanical filtration.

↓
These special balls, which can harbor many times more beneficial bacteria than under gravel filters, are placed inside trickle filters.

Ecology in Action: Biological Filtration

Biological filtration uses beneficial bacteria to break down the ammonia given off by fish food and fish waste (see The Nitrogen Cycle, right), a process similar to that used by municipal wastewater treatment facilities. The bacteria colonize the filters as well as areas inside the aquarium such as the gravel or substrate bottom. In saltwater reef aquariums, these bacteria are plentiful in the base rock used to build the reef structure on which the corals are eventually placed.

The purpose of a biological filter is to provide as much surface area as possible, in the least amount of space possible, on which the bacteria can colonize. It allows the bacteria to quickly and efficiently multiply—in effect, to catch up—as the fish and waste load of the aquarium increases.

The biological filter can take several forms and comprises the filter as well as the media or material inside the filter in which the bacteria establish colonies and multiply. This material can be specially shaped plastic balls, shredded PVC, or porous stones and other natural materials.

Types of Biological Filters

A vast array of filters is available; some are true biological filters, and some are filters or filtration devices that can serve as biological filters. Many of these are individual inventions or a company's variation on the tried-and-true principles of biological filtration. This book explores only the commonly used and more or less universally accepted dedicated biological filters—those generally used by professional aquarium installation and maintenance companies.

↓ ↘
Activated carbon is the most commonly used form of chemical filtration.

Undergravel Filters

Undergravel filters are probably the most recognized type of biological filter. Anyone who has visited a fish or pet shop can recall the unmistakable gurgling sound of bubbles ascending the undergravel filters' tall plastic tubes. Used mostly in freshwater aquariums and powered by either an air pump or a power head (a small motor that sits atop the plastic riser tubes), these filters pull aquarium water into the bacteria-laden gravel and then through a plastic plate with tiny holes in it. The bacteria catch the ammonia and nitrite molecules as they pass. The action of the rising air bubbles (or the pull of the power head motor) circulates the water back into the aquarium.

Although undergravel filters are effective and have been around a long time, they do have a few drawbacks. One challenge is concealing the plastic riser tube. Another is that the filter can pull debris into the gravel along with the water. If not removed, this debris accumulates and can eventually choke the system. The only way to remove the buildup is by siphoning or vacuuming the gravel bed. Simple, specialized vacuums are made for this purpose, but in tanks larger than about 150 gallons (567 liters), vacuuming can prove a real chore. Removing the decorative elements, vacuuming, and then resetting the aquascape is a lot of work and potentially stressful for the fish.

Regardless of who maintains the aquarium—you or an aquarium service—the easier it is to perform routine maintenance, the more likely it will be done and, in turn, the more consistent and stable the aquarium will be. So, while undergravel filters do have their place (small aquariums, retail fish stores, and quarantine or holding systems), today, better and more efficient options are available.

Aquarium Ecology

Biological filters provide the oxygen that aquarium bacteria need to feed, multiply, and thrive. Healthy bacteria break down fish wastes and other metabolic byproducts of the aquarium into less harmful chemicals. This process is known as the nitrogen cycle, and it forms the foundation for the ecology of every aquarium. Without delving too deeply into the hard science and headache-inspiring chemistry of this all-important process, a basic understanding of the cycle will help you understand what is going in your aquarium.

Two types of bacteria work together in your aquarium. One feeds on the primary toxin, ammonia (NH_4), which comes from fish food and fish feces, breaking it down into less toxic nitrite (NO_3). The second type of bacteria breaks down the nitrite into nitrate (NO_4), which, at low levels, is relatively harmless to fish. Because no bacteria feed on nitrate and no filter media readily remove it, the only way to eliminate it from the aquarium is by performing routine water changes.

The Nitrogen Cycle

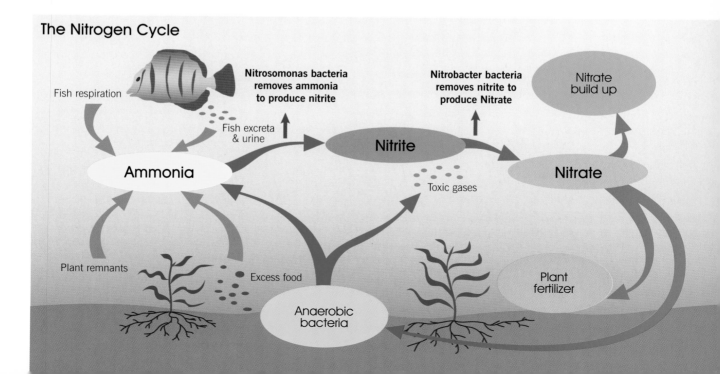

Fish respiration

Nitrosomonas bacteria removes ammonia to produce nitrite

Fish excreta & urine

Nitrobacter bacteria removes nitrite to produce Nitrate

Nitrate build up

Ammonia

Nitrite

Toxic gases

Nitrate

Plant remnants

Excess food

Anaerobic bacteria

Plant fertilizer

Trickle Filters

The trickle filter is so named because it trickles water over special filter media designed to generate beneficial nitrifying bacteria. The filter is commonly filled with specially shaped plastic balls, each harboring many square feet of bacteria. Whereas the under-gravel filter limits the amount of space available for colonizing bacteria to the surface area of the tank bottom, the trickle filter exponentially expands the available surface according to the amount of biological media used. It is far more efficient and capable of handling a greater bioload (the total amount of fish and subsequent waste produced).

Most trickle filters consist of an acrylic or glass box placed underneath the aquarium. The box houses the biological filter media and, in some cases, one or more sponges for additional mechanical filtration. It also has a sump or reservoir area in which water collects before being pumped back into the aquarium.

Aquariums made for use with trickle filters are designed with a built-in overflow box inside the aquarium. Water spills through tiny slats in the overflow box and runs into the filter below, then trickles through a drip plate filled with tiny holes and onto the biological media—that is, the specially shaped plastic balls. This trickle action keeps a constant mix of oxygen and water passing over the nitrifying bacteria.

A recirculation pump plumbed into the reservoir area returns the filtered water to the aquarium. It is important that this pump be properly rated to handle the volume of the particular aquarium size. In other words, the bigger the tank, the bigger the pump required to return the water from the sump to the aquarium.

In addition to its greatly increased surface area for bacteria, another benefit of the trickle filter is the lack of encumbrances, such as plastic tubes or hoses, interrupting the aquascape. Overflow boxes are typically placed in the corners of tanks and have an integrated appearance.

The trickle filter is standard for modern decorative saltwater aquariums. These aquariums benefit greatly from the rapid and efficient breakdown of waste toxins that trickle filters provide; excellent water quality is vital to keeping the saltwater aquarium's delicate inhabitants healthy. Of course, freshwater aquariums also benefit from this filter type, with the exception of some types of live-planted aquariums in which high oxygen levels can conflict with the carbon dioxide required to grow the plants. (See chapter 5 for more on this subject.)

Canister Filters

The most versatile of all filters is the canister filter. More canister filters find their way onto aquariums (especially large custom aquariums) than any other because they can serve as either a mechanical or biological filter (or both at the same time) and can house any chemical filter media. Although trickle filters are more efficient biological filters, for many freshwater aquariums, canister filters are up to the job.

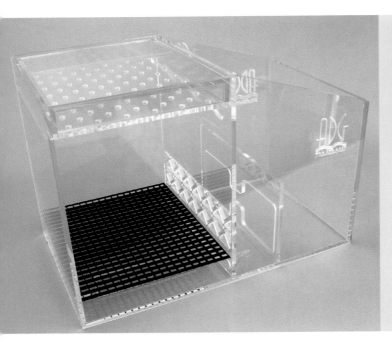

The ultimate utility of a canister filter is more a function of what media is used inside of it. One possibility is porous biological media for bacteria colonization combined with activated carbon for chemical filtration. The possibilities to target a specific water condition or chemistry are virtually limitless.

Canister filters come in many shapes and sizes, and multiples can be used when necessary. In fact, it is quite common to use two or more of these filters, so that one can be cleaned while the other continues to work. This is especially beneficial when the canister filter is used as the primary biological filter. Using two filters ensures that an established nitrifying bacteria colony constantly is filtering the waste load of the aquarium.

Although other filter maintenance techniques can minimize the loss of bacteria through cleaning, rinsing the canister's porous biological filter media with aquarium water (instead of tap or other water, which can shock or kill the bacteria) or removing a portion of the filter media and replacing them after the filter is cleaned are both workable methods. However, keeping one filter clean and one seamlessly performing its duty is preferable. Most professional installation and maintenance companies follow the two-canister model, even when only one is necessary to handle the given installation.

↑
Canister filters are available to fit aquariums of every size. Magnetic impeller-driven models tend to be the most reliable, and, as a rule, simple is the best when it comes to canister filtration. The fewer bells and whistles a canister filter offers, the better.

←
The acrylic trickle filter box is shown without biological media. The biological media is placed in the area below the top plate with holes, on top of the black grid (far left).

←
A trickle filter in service underneath an aquarium cabinet stand. The yellow arrow points to where the water flows from the aquarium's overflow box into the trickle filter (a). The green arrow points to a return pipe (b), which pumps water back into the aquarium. This return pipe runs up through the overflow box with an outflow inside the aquarium that returns the filtered water.

←
The yellow arrow points to the recirculation pump. Water is pulled from the sump area and (c) pumped back into the aquarium.

(c)

Chapter 4:
Lighting

Next to the composition or layout of the aquarium, the component with the greatest impact on aquarium appearance is lighting. The parallels between lighting an aquarium and lighting any other part of the home are obvious. Just as you would not want a brightly lit home theater or a dimly lit kitchen, you would not want too much or too little illumination on the aquarium. Just as you may include options for lighting extremes in either of the aforementioned spaces, you may desire the same for the aquarium—subdued and calm at times, bright and active at others.

Today's aquarium lighting options are many and varied. Nearly any look can be achieved with a good understanding of what is available and how to use it.

Fish Need Their Rest, Too!
Lighting Do's and Don'ts

Before discussing the specifics of light types and fixtures for the aquarium, let's review the basic rules of aquarium lighting. Following simple guidelines for amount of light (WPG, or watts per gallon) and amount of time the lights are on (known as the photoperiod) goes a long way toward minimizing algae growth and maintaining a consistently pleasing appearance in the aquarium.

Too Much, Not Enough, or Just Right:
Aquarium Lighting Basics

Some aquariums require more light than others. Most decorative aquariums (freshwater and saltwater aquariums that include only stones, wood, artificial plants, or decorative skeletal coral along with the fish) do not have a minimum light requirement. The choice of subdued or bright light is a matter of personal preference. On the other hand, live coral reef and live-planted aquariums have far greater light requirements because the lighting is used to stimulate and maintain the growth of the corals and/or plants. (See chapters 6 and 8 for more on this subject). Except in the case of live coral reef and live-planted aquariums, the amount of aquarium lighting used is not a major concern until the point of too much light is reached; for most decorative aquariums, this is anything more than about 2 WPG.

↑
Live-planted aquariums require intense lighting to grow the plants. The full-spectrum bulbs and high-wattage fixtures used can result in remarkable underwater scenes. Here, the angelfish appear to be ascending toward the heavens.

←
Direct sunlight can cause problems such as excessive algae growth, but diffused or indirect ambient light is seldom a problem. This aquarium takes advantage of the natural light that passes through the attached sunroom between the pool/patio and living room. Minimal aquarium-top lighting is still necessary, of course. Standard fluorescent fixtures get the job done here.

Although you can have more light on these tanks (see Daily Rhythms, page 41), more than 2 WPG encourages algae to grow on the glass and decorative elements.

The key to controlling excessive algae growth in aquariums in which more intense illumination is desired is to limit the total number of hours per day the lights are on (the photoperiod). If you are gone all day and no one is at home enjoying the aquarium, keep the lights off. As a rule, the shorter the photoperiod, the fewer the algae problems. Some days—weekends, for example—when the aquarium is in view or people are home all day, the lights can be on more. On other days, illumination should be kept to a minimum regardless of the light intensity. You certainly do not want to leave the lights on 24 hours a day or all night. This not only leads to algae problems but also prevents the fish from resting.

The Balancing Act:
Special Lighting Rules for
Reef and Live-Planted Aquariums

Live coral reef saltwater aquariums and freshwater live-planted aquariums are considered the pinnacles of aquarium keeping. True aquatic ecosystems, these aquarium styles require much special care and equipment. The tradeoff, though, is that when properly composed and maintained, they are visually stunning and color a space like nothing else. They define living art. A vital component for success with these sophisticated systems is the proper application of light. We explore the specifics of light requirements for live-planted and reef aquariums in chapters 6 and 8. For now, here are a few rules (and even a way or two around them) for lighting these beautiful systems.

Digital Timers and Remote Controls for Lighting

Two great ways to customize aquarium lighting and increase convenience are to add one or more digital timers and a simple remote control unit to the lighting system. Digital timers (as opposed to analog or rotary types) typically offer more programming features, such as a greater number of on/off cycles and the ability to switch lights on and off at varying times. Digital timers also have a backup battery (similar to a watch battery); in the event of a power failure, the timer keeps the correct time and restores the program cycle to normal when the power comes back on.

Using simple remote control units or tying the aquarium lights into your home lighting panels and controls makes it easy to turn aquarium lights on or off manually. For decorative aquariums with no photoperiod requirement, this may prove the best way to control lighting and enjoy the aquarium with the least potential for lights being left on too long.

An interesting side note: Some fish require time to wake up if the aquarium has been in total darkness for several hours. Incidental room light beyond the aquarium lighting is enough to keep fish active.

↓
Lighting is the key component for maintaining live corals. An aquarium like this one would not be possible without adequate light in the proper spectrum.

Daily Rhythms: The Photoperiod

The maximum amount of time per day that a reef or live-planted aquarium can be under full illumination is ten hours. There are always exceptions, but, for the most part, going even one or two hours beyond this prescribed ten-hour period can lead to problems, namely with algae and some corals and plants showing signs of distress. (The situation is comparable to our spending all day—and night—at the beach under the hot sun.) Full illumination simply is not an option for longer than the prescribed photoperiod or on an interval basis. Once on, the lights must stay on until it is time for them to go off, and vice versa.

You can enjoy these lovely aquariums outside the photoperiod, but carefully, as the dark cycle is almost as important to maintaining live coral and plants as the light cycle. One method is to include in your lighting system a standard-wattage fluorescent or power-compact fluorescent fixture that can be turned on independently and manually at specific times. Another is to attach a dedicated timer to a low-wattage fixture and program it to come on a few hours before or after the main photoperiod. This effectively extends the number of hours per day the lights are on, so that the aquarium can be enjoyed longer and can maintain a presence in the space.

Because the daily photoperiod of these aquariums is fixed, most people choose to program the aquarium lights to be on during the hours they are home. This varies from household to household. In the end, it does not matter if our nighttime is the reef aquarium's tropical midday sun. The important thing is to keep the lighting consistent and avoid keeping it on too long.

↓
A live coral reef aquarium just minutes after the lights have come on. The corals are just waking up and appear small, even shriveled, as they emerge from the long night.

↓
In five to six hours after the lights go on, under the simulation of a tropical midday sun, the corals are almost fully extended. This natural cycle should be taken into account when planning the optimal photoperiod for a coral reef aquarium.

Let There Be Light: Lighting Types and Fixtures for the Aquarium

Few system components affect the look of an aquarium like lighting. While some aquarium styles require specific lighting to function properly, most can be supplemented or customized to fit the viewing desires and times of the homeowner. Throughout the process of planning and designing the aquarium lighting system, consider functional versus aesthetic light, desired viewing times, and the special needs of the aquatic life.

Whether bright and vibrant or shadowy and subdued, the right lighting choices can yield any look. Two main lighting choices are available: fluorescent and halogen.

Basic Aquarium Lighting and More: Fluorescent Lighting

Fluorescent lighting has long been a staple for aquariums. Remember that aquarium with the long purplish bulb contained in a cheap-looking black plastic housing that sat in plain view atop the tank? From a pure function standpoint, these fixtures worked, but today we can do better, especially for custom installations and serious attempts to make the aquarium a design focal point.

↖

A strong white light added to the actinic 03 provides a brighter, more conventional lighting effect. Higher-spectrum bulbs, such as the 10,000 K, are strong enough to overcome the pure blue of the actinic 03 without completely eliminating the strong ocean water effect. This combination also can work well in freshwater aquariums.

←

Using a strong blue-spectrum bulb, known as an actinic 03, gives a very blue, deep marine appearance that is subdued and like the deeper ocean.

Standard-Wattage Fluorescents

Standard-wattage fluorescents are the classic fixture-and-bulb combinations that have been around for years. Available in 18-inch (46 cm), 24-inch (61 cm), 36-inch (91 cm), and 48-inch (122 cm) sizes, with corresponding wattages of 15, 20, 30, and 40, these can be considered low-wattage fixtures, especially when compared to the high-output units commonly used today. Standard fluorescent fixtures are suitable for smaller aquariums and production models from 10 to 75 gallons (38 to 284 liters), and more than one unit may be used for additional lighting needs. Standard fluorescents are great for providing subdued, low-algae-producing, aesthetic illumination for expanded viewing time beyond the day's normal photoperiod. For live-planted and coral reef aquariums, however, additional and more powerful lighting options are almost certainly necessary.

Many spectrums and color temperatures (known as Kelvin and symbolized by the letter K) are available to achieve a wide variety of effects and casts in the aquarium. From the higher color temperatures (up to 20,000 K), which are brighter and predominantly white and blue, to the lower temperatures (down to around 5,600 K), which are typically dimmer and predominantly red and yellow, it is possible to target a color range that both enhances fish color and flatters the aquascape.

Power-Compact Fluorescents

Power-compact fluorescents, or PCs, share many of the features of standard fluorescents but are much more intense at any given wattage. The reason is that the PC bulb is much smaller in diameter, so, powered by even similar wattage, the light is compressed into a smaller space. The result is a brighter and more pointed light than that produced by the larger-diameter tubes of standard fluorescents. A single PC fixture of the same physical size as its standard fluorescent counterpart is far brighter and more intense, which means that, instead of multiple fixtures needed to achieve a desired intensity, just one can handle the job.

The PC fixture gets much closer to a single-fixture option that is sufficient for smaller saltwater reef and freshwater live-planted aquariums. The PC is also a great choice for the main light source when you want to add a standard-wattage fixture to your lighting system for lower-light and extended viewing times. Most upper-end PC fixtures with more than one bulb have separate switches for each bulb or bulb set so they can be controlled independently. This opportunity for greater lighting flexibility allows you to put each switch on its own timer or power control point.

Power-compact bulbs are available in all spectrums and color temperatures. Be sure, however, to become familiar with the bulbs' pin patterns, located at the point where the bulb actually plugs into the fixture. Both straight and square pin arrangements are made, and bulbs of differing pin patterns are similarly packaged. Double-check the package labeling to be sure you have the right pin arrangement.

VHO and T5 Fluorescents

Other high-output fluorescents include very-high-output (VHO) fixtures and the recently introduced T5 fluorescent. Both are similar to power compacts and provide exceptional wattage and greater intensity in a single fixture. For example, whereas a 48-inch (122 cm) standard fluorescent bulb is 40 watts, a VHO of the same length is a whopping 120 watts! The decision to use these fixtures rather than other fluorescents may simply be based on availability or the suggestion of an aquarium professional. All the fluorescent fixtures beyond the classic standard-wattage sizes are just different means to the same end: brighter light.

Design Tip

Mix-and-Match Bulbs

Using bulbs of the same spectrum does not always render the best appearance. Mix and match spectrums to create the desired look in the aquarium. Choose fixtures that have two or more bulbs each, or add additional fixtures. One popular combination is a 10,000 K (very white, intense midday-sun-type) bulb with a special ultra-blue-spectrum bulb known as an actinic or actinic 03. Even at high wattages, the actinic 03 is quite subdued in intensity and in effect just mellows the much more intense 10,000 K (referred to also as 10 K). Both bulbs are designed for functional application on live coral reef aquariums but can be used for purely aesthetic purposes on decorative saltwater and freshwater aquariums. The combined light cast is flattering to most tropical fish, often bringing out blues and deep iridescences.

Lighting Control Panels

Incorporate your aquarium lighting into custom lighting systems through wall-mounted control panels. This provides easier access and on-demand lighting control for the aquarium as well as the rest of the room. Most professional lighting installers can take care of this. Meet with your professional lighting designer or installer ahead of time to discuss this option. Show the designer the fixtures to be integrated so he or she can determine compatibility and necessary modifications.

Shimmering Rays

A gorgeous application for halogen lighting is to use a single fixture in conjunction with a fluorescent source. Use the fluorescents for the main or functional light, and position the halogen fixture over a focal point in the aquascape, off a corner, or simply centered over the aquarium. The halogen fixture provides a focused area of shimmering light, much like the Sun's rays beaming through the water, casting shadows and conveying a sense of a natural underwater scene.

→
This look is achieved with only fluorescent fixtures, giving a constant, even distribution of light across the aquascape.

→
Adding a single pendant-type metal halide fixture creates a ray of light down the midsection of the aquascape. While difficult to capture in a photograph, this ray of light actually shimmers beneath the current and looks like a sunbeam stretching into the aquarium. It adds a wonderful emphasis to the layout focal points.

→
The single metal halide fixture alone creates a strong contrast of light and shadow—excellent when a more subdued appearance is desired.

Halogen Lighting

The other major type of aquarium lighting is halogen, or metal halide. Halogen light has a shorter wavelength than fluorescent light, which is the source of its ability to project rays of light into the aquarium for a beautifully natural look. The generally higher wattage and spectrums that interact with the water are more like natural sunlight, making halogen lighting a top choice and near-standard application for live reef and live-planted aquariums.

HQI Halogens

Imagine taking the light of several regular bulbs and compressing it into a tiny sliver of glass that fits in the palm of your hand. Because of the massive compression, the intensity of the light is far greater, and the bulb's ability to penetrate water is greatly increased. This is the concept behind the HQI metal halide lamp. The comparison between larger-diameter metal halide bulbs and HQI bulbs is similar to that between standard-wattage fluorescents and power-compact fluorescents. For the same wattage, light from an HQI bulb is much more intense and pointed, so a single fixture can house fewer bulbs and still provide the necessary wattage and intensity.

In fact, these lamps can be so intense that it is almost standard to mix them with other types of light (power-compact fluorescents are a popular choice). While these intense lights convey significant functional benefits, such as growing vigorous plants and corals (remember: they are much more like natural sunlight), they are often too intense to be run all day or for the full duration of the photoperiod. Over a ten-hour photoperiod, for example, metal halides are run, on average, for six to eight hours.

Most standard color temperatures are available, with the higher Kelvin ratings (blues and whites) being somewhat more common, because these fixtures are so often used for saltwater applications in which those spectrums are necessary. Lower Kelvin ratings (yellows, reds, and greens) for freshwater, live-planted aquariums are available too, however, and are enjoying ever-increasing popularity.

Pendant-Style Metal Halide Fixtures

Pendant-style fixtures are usually suspended from the ceiling over open-top aquariums. They are a great way to get good intensities at greater depths within the aquarium from a fixture that is ultimately quite high above the water surface. These fixtures allow for plenty of from-above viewing, the unique feature of open-top aquariums. Pendant fixtures also make excellent accent lights for aquariums with other lighting systems.

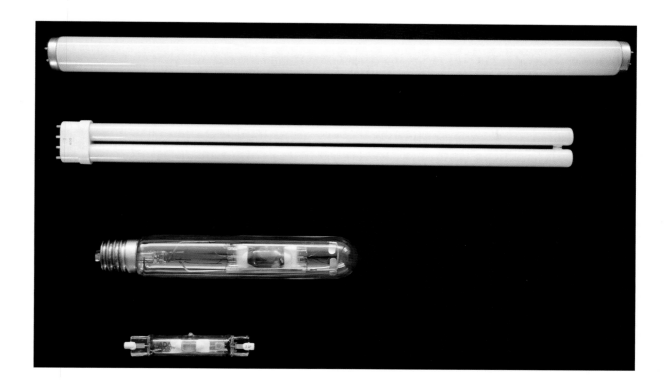

↑
From top to bottom: standard fluorescent bulb; power-compact (PC) fluorescent; standard-type metal halide (halogen) bulb; HQI halogen.

↖
Height adjustability is a real advantage of pendant fixtures. This shallow coral reef aquarium requires strong light for the corals to grow, but most fixtures that would be placed directly on top of such an aquarium would either be too strong or not strong enough. The ability to raise them to an exact desired height allows the light intensity to be made just right.

Design Tip

Moon Lights
As LED light technologies have advanced, applications for everything from ultrabright pocket flashlights and automotive effects lighting to—you guessed it— aquariums have emerged. LED-based moon lights are the rage among aquarists for their distinctive moon-glow effect. These lights cast a nighttime illumination on the aquarium. Observe the after-dark behaviors of fish and corals, many of which are most active at night, for a whole new viewing experience. These LEDs are now incorporated into many fixtures as an added feature or can be purchased and installed separately.

Freshwater aquariums can be divided into two major styles: decorative and live-planted. Although both styles are in the freshwater category, the needs, equipment, and maintenance requirements for each are so dissimilar that they can be viewed as different systems altogether. Decorative freshwater aquariums are composed of hardscape materials only, such as stones and driftwood and artificial plants, while live-planted freshwater aquariums use living aquatic plants for the aquascape, and much emphasis is placed on the needs of the plants. That is not to say the fish are not an important component of the live-planted aquarium, but the care of the aquarium centers around the growth and management of the plants.

Both freshwater styles offer the potential to complement a space with a softer aesthetic than their saltwater counterparts. This aesthetic can be compared to the differences between, for example, a landscape painting and a brightly colored abstract work. Either could function within a variety of décors, or even the same décor, but one is likely to work better than the other.

As the availability of colorful and exotic freshwater fishes has increased, so have the possibilities for creating beautiful and inspired freshwater aquariums. Great progress has been made in the design of these aquariums, which were long neglected in favor of the saltwater aquarium's instant impact and showiness. Factor in the minimal equipment requirements with the significantly lower cost and greater availability of hardy fish species, and a freshwater aquarium becomes an attractive alternative with a lot of design versatility.

←

A calming world of green tones defines this 220-gallon (832 liter) freshwater live-planted aquarium. Using plants that require infrequent trimming is the key to this composition's potential for long-term sustainability. Such an aquascape could be paired with many interior styles.

Chapter 5:
Decorative Freshwater Aquariums

The use of artificial plants and various types of stone or driftwood defines the decorative freshwater aquarium. By far the easiest to maintain and the most versatile style to design, decorative freshwater aquariums rival saltwater aquariums in popularity and even surpass them in affordability. The reasons are simple: These aquariums require the least amount of equipment (and therefore investment) of any aquarium style, and they offer myriad design possibilities. The result is an installation that complements and harmonizes with a room while offering the low stress and peace of mind of an exceedingly simple installation and life-support system.

Natural elements, such as rock, river stone, petrified wood, and driftwood, can be used alone or in combination with an enormous variety of attractive and realistic-looking artificial plants to create aquascapes that help the aquarium extend the design theme or overall feel of a room. The aquascape can be bold and bright, with large groups of colorful ornamental fish swimming and interacting, or subtle and subdued, with limited species set against a minimalist composition of stones and branches.

Decorative Freshwater Design Possibilities

It is important to realize the effect a given style of aquarium can have on your space. Think for a moment of the difference between a rain forest streambed and a coral reef—each projects a different sense of nature's art. When one of these realms is captured in an aquarium, it projects that sense into the room.

↗

A pleasing composition with accents in all the right places, this aquarium inspires quiet contemplation from the many surrounding seating areas.

←

A delightful 80-gallon (303-liter) decorative freshwater aquarium.

→

A whimsical composition using freshwater parrot cichlids was used for this 100-gallon (378-liter) decorative freshwater aquarium.

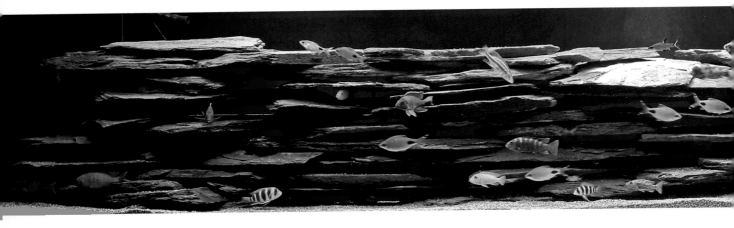

The decorative freshwater aquarium's aesthetic versatility is due, in part, to our ideas about what a freshwater environment looks like, coupled with the wealth of compositional elements available. Our notion of what the ocean looks like—the fishes, corals, and blue water—is more clearly defined. The freshwater environment is suggestive of nature, and an infinite variety of natural aquascapes can be created with stones, substrates, and artificial plants. The many colors, sizes, and behaviors of available freshwater fish greatly expand the palette and offer even more design opportunities for the aquarium. This enables a homeowner or designer to think in terms of decorating with the aquarium—integrating into the home not just the installation and cabinetry but also the aquarium's interior contents and composition.

From the most contemporary to the most traditional design aesthetic—and every eclectic combination thereof—you can develop an application for the decorative freshwater aquarium. It is simply a matter of understanding the relationship of the aquarium and the surrounding décor, and the extent to which harmony between the two is a priority.

↑
The stacked slate technique used in this 96 × 30 × 24-inch (245 × 75 × 61 cm), 300-gallon (1,135-liter) aquarium conveys a contemporary design sensibility. A composition like this is exceedingly easy to maintain.

Layout Styles

With all the potential design approaches available for the decorative freshwater aquarium, how do you go about determining which one will work best for your application? Let's look at the two most common layout styles—hardscape only and designs using artificial plants—and get a feel for how they work within the space and provide for the needs of the fish.

Simplicity Defined: Hardscape-Only Designs
The simplest design approach limits the compositional elements to rockwork, driftwood, or a combination of the two. Even artificial plants are excluded in favor of creating a minimal, easy-to-maintain aquascape. Often, the hardscape structure

Harmonizing Colors with Stones and Substrates
Look for stones with neutral colors or tones that are similar to carpet or tile in the space. Keep an eye out for design cues in artwork, furniture, or anything in the room that offers an opportunity to play off a color. The substrate (gravel, sand, etc.) is also an excellent medium with which to imbue a sense of harmony, as almost any color, size, and texture of material can be obtained. You can find everything from powdery white sand to large, round river pebbles, each offering its own unique mood to both the aquascape and the space.

need not be moved or disturbed for maintenance and water changes. As a result, when properly executed, the hardscape-only layout can really settle in, conveying a sense of permanence—as if it has existed naturally through the passage of time.

One advantage of a design that uses no artificial plants is ease of maintenance. In most aquariums, unless the light source is very dim, artificial plants acquire algae—usually a powdery brown variety—that quickly becomes unsightly unless regularly cleaned. While algae can also grow on rocks and driftwood, it is not as visible. In fact, over time, algae give a nice natural patina to rock and actually enhance its appearance.

This layout style also the most suitable for many fish species because few or no aquatic plants exist in their natural environment. Creating a rock or slate backdrop with the requisite cracks and crevices for these fish to engage in their natural behaviors can prove effective, as many show better color as result of feeling at home. You can often add a greater number of fish to these layouts that provide fish places to establish territories.

↑
The reds and greens of these artificial plants create a splendid backdrop for the colorful fishes. Short grass in the foreground and tall, thin background plants add depth to this 72 × 30 × 30-inch (183 × 75 × 75 cm), 240-gallon (910-liter) decorative freshwater aquarium.

Easy Nature: Using Artificial Plants
You can produce a surprisingly natural-looking aquascape by using artificial plants in your aquarium design. In fact, thanks to great advances in the manufacture of these botanical imitators, many look so lifelike that they readily pass for the real thing.

You can find a wide range of simulated species in all heights, types, and sizes to create limitless combinations. Use giant-sized types to fill in backgrounds and conceal filtration components and miniatures for detail work and filling in the foreground. The key to a great design is to choose plants wisely. It is possible to work with artificial aquarium plants in much the same way one works with terrestrial plants, both real and faux: with an eye for using complementary and contrasting species to achieve a pleasing, balanced look.

Design Tip

Working with Rocks
When creating a rock layout, develop a varied and natural aquascape by incorporating as many sizes as possible. Place the largest, or lead, stones prominently and accompany them with medium and smaller stones. Use the smallest stones in the foreground and for detail work. Try creating families of stones, and imbue a sense of random order in which the rocks appear to have come together by natural forces. Be sure, however, to convey a sense of balance and proportion. For a natural appearance, avoid placing stones of similar size in rows or overly contrived patterns.

Keeping It Simple:
Decorative Freshwater System Design

The minimal nature of the typical decorative freshwater aquarium system allows for lower initial investment, easier installation, and more time spent enjoying the aquarium than worrying about equipment monitoring or failure. These facts build a strong case for the decorative freshwater aquarium as ideal for people who don't have the option or desire to hire a professional installation and maintenance service or who just want to keep it simple.

Filtration

An immensely attractive component of the decorative freshwater aquarium is the straightforward nature of the filtration and system components. In most instances, simple canister filtration is more than adequate for filtration. It can be easily plumbed through the bottom of the aquarium, and the filter intakes and outflows are concealed by the aquascape. Trickle filters may also be used, generally in addition to canister filters.

Lighting

Options for lighting the decorative freshwater aquarium are limitless. Because the light need not address the demands of growing plants or living corals, it is possible to use fluorescents, halogens, or a combinations of the two. The designer is free to use light to create any mood at all, from bright and shimmering to shadowy and subdued. Running different light sources or combinations at different times of the day to achieve varying looks within the aquarium is seldom a problem and contributes to design flexibility.

↑
(Top) A single large-capacity canister filter like this one can easily handle a 200-gallon (757-liter) aquarium. Include a small air pump for added or backup aeration; it just doesn't get any easier! In this setup, the inflow and outflow are plumbed through the bottom via predrilled holes in the aquarium/support stand and bulkhead fittings.

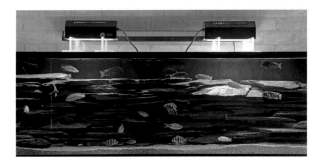

↑
With the canopy removed, we see that two pendant-style halogen light fixtures, supported by custom-made acrylic bases, provide ample light for this aquarium, although other fluorescent fixtures types could be easily added. Here, the homeowner prefers the light and shadow contrast created by just the two pendants.

Design Tip

In-Line Heaters

Most decorative freshwater aquariums benefit from a heater that keeps the water at a constant temperature. Traditionally, the heater went inside the aquarium, forming another encumbrance to conceal. Using an external in-line heater eliminates this problem, because the heater module is inside the aquarium cabinetry. It is installed in line with the aquarium canister filter, and the filtered water passes through the heater before returning to the aquarium.

Bringing the Outside In

For aquariums installed near windows or in areas in which the outside landscaping is visible (through the aquarium or an alternate view, for instance), look for layout materials that play off the outdoor elements. Rocks and plants with a look similar to those outside express a relationship between indoor and outdoor elements.

↑
The influence of the outside trees can be felt in this decorative freshwater scene. The view through the window forms a natural background for the aquarium, whose design was intentionally left open on the back side. Stonework around the swimming pool similarly complements the aquarium rocks.

The Fish

We have addressed layout styles, composition, and other means of elevating the aesthetics of the aquarium. Now, we shift our attention to the most important component of all: the fish. A huge palette of fish species is available for the decorative freshwater aquarium; with them, you can create a virtually endless number of underwater scenes. The fish obviously play the lead role in the aquascape and are the first things most people look at when viewing the aquarium. Providing life and movement, color and character, the fish are what make the aquarium such a special fixture, one that is more than a mere design element.

While a comprehensive index of every possible species and their accompanying behaviors, condition requirements, and other specifics is beyond the scope of this book, we here look at some of the major groups suitable for the freshwater decorative aquarium and explore ways to harmonize the fish with the aquascape. This approach provides basic guidelines for selecting fish for the decorative freshwater aquarium and gives a sense of interspecies compatibility and other important concerns.

Freshwater Kaleidoscope: African Cichlids

One of the most popular groups of freshwater fish is the cichlids. While cichlid species can be found all over the world, some of the most colorful come from the massive rift lakes of Africa, especially Lake Malawi. Although species are collected and bred regionally from nearby lakes Tanganyika and Victoria, fish from those lakes are rarer and typically considered collector fish.

↑
A large group of African cichlids from Lake Malawi enjoys the craggy rockwork.

The extremely rocky, craggy underwater environment of the lakes in which the African cichlids evolved provides ideal conditions for them to exercise their territorial nature and has given rise to hundreds of distinct yet related species. Their prolific nature, combined with a hardy and voracious temperament, has made African cichlids a staple in the aquarium trade for decades, and they can be found in practically every retail fish store worldwide. They are not picky eaters, adapt quickly to a wide range of water conditions, and several species rival saltwater fish for color and grace.

Aquascaping with African Cichlids: Aesthetics and Behavior

Most African cichlids, especially the colorful varieties, are aggressive, territorial fish and are generally not compatible with peaceful fish—guppies, for example. For this reason, they require a large enough aquarium for the fish to stake their individual claims.

In the aquarium, the average adult size for most Lake Malawi African cichlids is about 4 to 6 inches (10 to 15 cm), but some can grow a bit larger. Starting out with a large group of similarly sized juveniles in the 1 to 2-inch (2.5 to 5 cm) range helps avoid the emergence of a single dominant fish that perpetually antagonizes smaller and weaker fish. This approach also helps spread a dominant individual's aggression over many fish, so no single or pair of weaker individuals bears all of the aggression. It is a natural way to balance African cichlids' territorial nature.

Aggressive as they are, it is possible to keep many of these vivacious fish with other tropical, noncichlid species. Though many purists argue against mixing African cichlids with tropical fish, a number of species show exceptional compatibility with other varieties of freshwater fish.

↗

The lemon yellow Labidichromis is a peaceful cichlid that is compatible with many other freshwater fish (top).

↗

The electric blue Aulonocara is as striking in coloration as many saltwater fish.

↗

A red-top Fuliborni. Orange is often called red in the naming of African cichlids. The orange dorsal fin of this blue fish adds to its appeal.

→

The sunshine peacock has a mild temperament and adds a splash of color to aquariums that include tropical fish and other noncichlid species. These two are males. Females are not nearly as colorful as the males, which is true of most African cichlid species.

→

A deep navy blue color characterizes the Demasoni (left).

→

The red zebra is a classic African cichlid. It spawns quite readily in the aquarium, and offspring can quickly overpopulate it. Red zebras are also prone to digging in the substrate, as are all Pseudotropheus species, of which the red zebra is a prominent member.

→

The snow-white Soccolofi provides excellent contrast in the cichlid aquarium, though it is prone to digging.

Foremost among the compatible cichlids is the yellow Labidochromis. Characterized by its bright lemon-yellow coloration, this fish shows perhaps the least aggressive or territorial nature of all the commonly used African cichlids. They have been known to cohabitate with even the most peaceful of freshwater fishes—as long as the other fish are too large to fit into their mouths. Other African cichlids of comparatively mild temperament include many of the Aulonochara species, also known as peacocks—the electric blue and sunshine peacock among them—for their bright and brilliant coloration. Although these fish show fewer negative traits than other African cichlids, they are still aggressive enough to warrant seeking advice about potential tankmates. In other words, if you are unsure about the compatibility of an African cichlid species with another type of fish, consult a local fish retailer, your aquarium maintenance company, or an online source.

Another consideration, from an aquascaping standpoint, is that many African cichlids dig into the substrate, especially when fine gravel or sand is used. To some extent, the digging is just part of keeping these fish. If you care strongly about maintaining a level gravel line, plan to frequently smooth it out by hand.

It is important to take into careful consideration the behavioral tendencies of these fish—their highly active and downright voracious tendencies—and their effects on the aquarium as a whole, especially when they are in large groups. Cichlids do not swim peacefully about the aquarium, and the competition among tankmates for prime territories can become quite fierce, so you need to decide on the level of activity and interaction you desire in the aquarium. For many, studying cichlid territorial struggles and observing the lively swimming patterns provide the excitement and pleasure they seek in an aquarium. For others, this can be not only undesirable but also stressful, which defeats the purpose of having an aquarium.

African cichlids make a striking aquarium display, whether kept alone or with other freshwater fish. Keeping a few select species among other types of freshwater fish bring to the aquarium their beauty and positive attributes while minimizing their less desirable traits.

Design Tip

Designing with African Cichlids
Because African cichlids share a common ancestor and have remained confined to the same body of water for thousands of years, they generally have a similar shape and temperament. For this reason, be sure to consider their comparative uniformity—mostly of body shape—when planning to include them in an aquarium with other tropical fish species or (especially) when executing a cichlid-only display.

The Living Palette: Freshwater Tropical Fish

The number and variety of tropical freshwater fish suitable for the aquarium is astounding. In addition to the popular African cichlids are beautiful and interesting species from every tropical region of the globe. Two major sources for commonly seen tropical fish are Southeast Asia and South America; most of the noncichlid fish available are from these regions.

Today, most popular tropical fish are bred in large tropical fish hatcheries rather than collected from the wild. Captive-bred fish have a number of advantages over wild-caught fish, the major one being that they have not been pulled from a natural environment, handled, shipped—possibly many times—and then handled some more before finally reaching your aquarium. Captive-bred fish pass through fewer hands and fewer changing water conditions, which means they are in better condition when you buy them. Disease resistance and other health factors are typically better with captive-raised fish.

Rainbow Fishes
Native to Australia, New Guinea, and Indonesia, rainbows are a varied group of freshwater fish whose many species boast wonderful, vibrant colors. Their peaceful nature keeps them high on the list of popular tropical fish, and most of the best color varieties are readily available throughout the year.

Rainbows mix well with species of varied temperaments, and their swimming patterns range from swift and deliberate to hovering and languid. But it is their distinctive shape that sets them apart and provides a nice contrast to other fish in the aquarium. Typically not finicky eaters, they eat most common fish foods, such as flakes, small pellets, and frozen foods. While they can be on the delicate side when first introduced into a new aquarium, with good water quality and otherwise stable conditions, they settle in nicely after a few weeks. Established adults can live for many years.

Design Tip

Neutral Beauty:
Use of Muted-Color Fish in the Aquascape
When it comes to tropical fish, color is not always everything. While there is a strong tendency toward wanting fish of the most dazzling colors possible, sometimes a neutral tone can have greater effect. One way to enhance and draw attention to the most colorful fish in an aquascape is to add one or more varieties of a muted-color fish to the group. Many freshwater fish that are not themselves brightly colored provide a nice counterpoint to the fish that are more colorful. These fish often contribute a different shape to the scene as well.

Good examples of muted-color fish are tinfoil barbs and silver dollars. These mostly silver fish exhibit nice swim patterns, are hardy, and provide another layer to the aquarium community. The red hook is a muted-color fish with just a splash of color. It is similar to the silver dollar but has a subtle yet eye-catching red lower fin.

↑
A scene from a decorative freshwater aquarium dominated by active and colorful rainbow fishes. These fish are similar in general shape, but true to their namesake, they exist in a veritable rainbow of colors—blues, reds, yellows, and diverse patterns.

↑
Multiple species of cichlids, barbs, and freshwater sharks cohabitate peacefully in this decorative freshwater aquarium.

↑
Yellow Axelrodi rainbow

↑
Boesmani rainbow

↑
Red Irian rainbow

↑
Praecox rainbow

Freshwater Sharks and Loaches

Most commonly available freshwater sharks and loaches come from Southeast Asia and surrounding regions. Although the name sounds exciting, freshwater sharks are not related to saltwater sharks. They are, however, similarly shaped—all feature the characteristic high dorsal (top) fin—and the many varieties add this shape to the aquarium scene. Their swim pattern is neither especially skittish nor leisurely. They do well on all the common fish foods and are typically hardy, peaceful (no chance of being attacked—promise!), and easily acquired. A few species, such as red-tailed sharks and rainbow sharks, should be kept only one to an aquarium; with two, the more dominant individual almost always antagonizes the other.

Closely related to many of the freshwater sharks, loaches (also known as Botias) are another fascinating and appealing aquarium inhabitant. Many people are familiar with the clown loach (*Botia macracanthus*), with its tiger stripes and distinctive red fins. The clown loach can be thought of as the diplomat of the aquarium in that it is compatible with virtually every tropical fish, from the peaceful to the most aggressive. They do best in small groups and stay together as they scurry about the aquarium bottom.

Clown loaches are also an excellent control for natural-nuisance snails. Many types of snails can mysteriously appear in the aquarium. While a few incidental snails can be charming, if left unchecked, their populations can explode and quickly become unsightly—imagine so many snails that the gravel bottom appears to move! Fortunately, small snails are a favorite food of the clown loach and most other common Botias, and they typically prevent what starts out as a few cute snails from taking over the aquarium.

↑
The rose-line shark is a striking freshwater fish that is particularly impressive in groups of five or more.

↓
Clown loaches and Botias frollicking together. Both loach species are more active when kept in groups. Kept alone or in pairs, they tend to hide most of the time.

South American Cichlids

Another group of fishes that have remained popular through the years are the cichlids of South America. Perhaps most notable among them is the oscar, a fish with a remarkable petlike quality in that, over time, it seems to get to know its owners, and many have been known to accept being touched or even petted on the head! They are, indeed, a fish with character.

Red or tiger oscars can be obtained as juveniles from almost any major fish and aquarium store or supplier. Many people make the mistake of buying baby oscars and putting them in a 10- to 20-gallon (38- to 76 liter) tank, which they quickly outgrow, so adult sizes of every range are also available. As a rule, you need an aquarium size of 100 gallons (378 liters) or larger to grow oscars and many of the other popular South American cichlids. To maintain a seriously impressive display of these fish, an aquarium of 200 gallons (757 liters) or more is generally required.

Other well-known species of South American cichlids include the green terror, the firemouth cichlid, and the ever-popular Jack Dempsey. These species include members that, like the oscar,

→

A group of South American fishes enjoying a large aquarium. The diversity of compatible species from the Amazon region is immense. Shapes, colors, and behaviors abound, forming an intriguing community of large tropical fish.

↓

All the fish in this 96 × 30 × 30-inch (244 × 76 × 76 cm), 375-gallon (1,419 liter) decorative freshwater aquarium are from South America, and most are found in or near the Amazon River. The aquascape incorporates bulky pieces of driftwood to give the feel of a flooded forest, which is a natural occurrence each year in the Amazon during the rainy season.

either grow quite large—10 to 12 inches (25 to 30 cm) or more!—or need a large aquarium to peacefully coexist with their territorial and fairly aggressive tankmates.

Most South American cichlids are hardy fish and require only the most basic care in terms of water-change frequency, system design, and diet. It is possible to compose quite a cast of characters from this group because so many of the fish have strong and distinctive personalities. As is true with most fish, the males are usually the more colorful, and acquiring male and female pairs of many species is relatively easy. While spawns within the aquarium are a fairly common occurrence, the eggs or the fry often are eaten by the other fish—although for the first day or so after eggs are laid, the parents put on quite a show in trying to protect them by flaring fins, showing stronger color, and engaging in the occasional head-butt with a would-be attacker. These activities are generally benign, but watch aggressive behaviors closely in case they become more serious. While this is true for all fish, it is particularly so with these large cichlid species, whose persistent aggressive behavior can result in real problems and even fish death.

↑
A small group of albino tiger barbs (top). Many common tropical fish species include an albino member, usually developed through the selective breeding practices of tropical fish hatcheries.

↑
The pretty-finned river barb can also be sold as a type of freshwater shark.

→
The German-bred koi angelfish is one of many angelfish hybrids. As with so many other freshwater tropicals, the impact of the fish is heightened when they are kept in a group.

A Fish for Every Need: Other Useful and Popular Tropical Fish

Tropical fish species are far too numerous to list and explore in this book. Books, magazines, and online sources for in-depth and specific information about tropical fish abounds. But a few more species are worth noting for their distinctive character and affable appeal within the aquarium. Some of the species explored in the next chapter on freshwater live-planted aquariums also work well for decorative freshwater aquarium and are so noted.

> **Barbs**

Barbs are a lively little group of fish considered semiaggressive in temperament. Active and fairly voracious, they may nip at the fins of their mellower tankmates, though they are generally not too antagonistic to be compatible with a wide range of species. The ever-popular tiger barb and its hybridized cousin, the green barb, as well as the rosy barb (both regular and long-finnedvarieties) are easy to find and look great in medium-sized groups of at least 10 to 15 individuals.

> **Angelfish**

Most people are familiar with the elegant and beautiful angelfish. Although not colorful in the traditional sense, the angelfish is admired for its unusual vertical shape and elongated top and bottom fins. Angelfish are native to South America, where they are still collected and shipped around the world, but many varieties—both natural and hybrid forms—are now captive-bred.

Actually a type of South American cichlid, large specimens can be a bit aggressive and territorial. A good strategy for minimizing these behaviors when keeping angelfish in a community setting is to acquire them as small as possible and raise them in the aquarium with the other species. When raised this way, they are compatible with many types of fish. They typically cohabitate peacefully with other species if the aquarium is of suitable size and the other fish do not fit into the angelfish's relatively small mouth.

> **Catfish**

Dozens of catfish species can be kept successfully in the aquarium. Most catfish are exclusively bottom-dwellers and add dimension to the fish display by occupying the lower regions of the aquarium, where mid- and top-water fish seldom spend much time. Most species are also good scavengers and helpfully clean up food that settles to the bottom, though periodic target feeding of sinking foods may be necessary. Aquarium-friendly catfish varieties can be found all over the world; most are neither aggressive nor territorial, but some may grow very large and eventually outgrow the aquarium.

↑
The spotted bushy-nose pleco is an excellent algae eater.

→
The parrotfish in this decorative freshwater aquarium are not only adding their quirky charm to the display, their orange coloration is helping harmonize the aquarium with the reds and orange tones of the furniture.

> *Plecostomus* (algae eaters)

The *Plecostomus*, or suckermouth, is one of the most useful fish for the decorative freshwater aquarium. While other fish also eat algae, the many *Plecostomus* species (often called plecos for short) are by far the most common and popular. Most help keep stones and other decorative elements clean, but a few have proven especially beneficial in this regard, particularly the bushy-nose varieties. So named for an unusual growth on the tips of their heads, these plecos tend to stay small—4 to 6 inches (10 to 15 cm)—unlike the more common *Plecostomus* species sold as juveniles at 2 inches (5 cm) or so; these can reach lengths of more than 15 inches (38 cm)!

While common plecos are initially good algae eaters, after reaching 8 to 10 inches (20 to 25 cm), they seem to produce more visible waste than they clean up. No fish kept in the aquarium eats the waste of other fish, and it is a myth that plecos do this. It is also worth noting that, while many of the specialty or collector varieties can be delightful additions to the aquarium, they may not prove as good at keeping the aquarium décor clean.

> Parrotfish

International fish hatcheries have a long tradition of genetically crossing species of related fish to create entirely new varieties to introduce into the aquarium fish trade. Many are dismissed as mere novelties, but one man-made hybrid has gained enormous popularity and gone on to become a common character in fish shops and hobbyists' aquariums alike. The parrotfish, or parrot-cichlid, is a cross between two South American cichlids: the red devil and the gold severum. So named for their faces, which resemble a parrot's beak, these fish possess a cartoonlike quality and can introduce an animated and whimsical note to the aquarium.

> Fancy Goldfish

Varieties of fancy goldfish have been kept in bowls and aquariums for centuries, their popularity due in large part to their bizarre and often exaggerated features and their almost iconic association with Asian aesthetics. Actually a coldwater fish, the goldfish's metabolism is quite fast. As a result, it tends to produce waste more quickly than other fish and should therefore be fed only foods intended specifically for goldfish.

Due to their preference for cooler water and need for special foods, goldfish should be kept only with other goldfish. Mixing in tropical freshwater fish can compromise the long-term health of one or the other sort. Water quality can be an issue with goldfish aquariums due to the waste factor, so supplemental filtration is advised to reduce the need for constant water changes. Otherwise, fancy goldfish are quite hardy and positively entertaining to watch as they bob and shimmy about the aquarium.

↑
This aquascape offers an idyllic setting for fancy goldfish. The stonework consists of four grades of Mexican beach pebble. The smooth, round stones accent the round shape of the fish.

Keep It Clean: Maintenance Guidelines for the Decorative Freshwater Aquarium

For most of us, the easier a task is to perform, the more likely it is to get done regularly. This certainly proves true with respect to aquarium maintenance; how much time we are willing to allocate to it influences the beauty and long-term health of the aquarium. Ease of maintenance is without doubt one of the biggest benefits of decorative freshwater aquariums. Except for the addition of a little dechlorinator, not much is required for water conditioning, and in most regions and with most fish types, tap water is just fine for routine water changes.

Water Changes

Most types of decorative freshwater aquariums do just fine with once-a-month water changes, although some aquarists prefer more frequent changes, even for the long term, and subscribe to a biweekly protocol. A newly set up aquarium also needs more frequent, smaller water changes until it is completely cycled and stable.

The big question: How much water should be changed each month? While no definitive answer applies to all systems, a safe minimum starting point is 30 to 50 percent. This varies depending on the type and capacity of the filtration system, fish-stocking levels, and, perhaps most important, the amount food given each day.

Most aquarium maintenance companies have a good feel for what a given system requires and likely have preset or prescribed regimens for various aquarium styles. When handling your own maintenance, let observation be your guide. Start with the 50-percent-per-month rule and gauge from there whether to change more or less water. In the end, most aquariums benefit from more frequent, smaller-volume water changes. Some aquarists even change water every few days, but usually for specific reasons, such as husbandry of rare or delicate species or attempting to induce spawning. The goal is to strike a balance between the needs of the aquarium, the homeowner's desired presentation level, and the time or budget available for routine maintenance.

Filters

Filter maintenance is, by far, more subjective than water changes. Many theories exist about the type of media to use and how often (if ever) it should be changed or the filter cleaned. Many factors can affect how often filters must be cleaned, and there are no set rules when it comes to questions of frequency. For the most part, biological filtration should not be disturbed too often because it disrupts the ecological balance of the aquarium (see The Nitrogen Cycle, page 35). Using only aquarium water to rinse out biological filter media helps keep more of the precious nitrifying bacteria intact.

All forms of mechanical filters can usually be cleaned often but may not necessarily require cleaning for the aquarium water to remain clear. The appearance of cloudy water resulting from suspended particulate or debris is a good sign that the filter needs cleaning.

↑
A large-diameter drain/siphon hose can be routed to a nearby toilet or built-in drain hole to quickly remove water from the aquarium.

↑
Clamps like this are available at hardware stores and work well to hold hoses in place.

↑
A strainer attached to the end of the drain hose prevents accidentally sucking up fish!

Cleaning Artificial Plants

The best way to clean most plastic artificial plants is to soak them in a mild solution of bleach and water. Rinse thoroughly, then soak in clean water with a generous amount of dechlorinator and rinse again thoroughly before returning the plants to the aquarium. Another method is to run the plants through the dishwasher for one cycle using no detergent. Be sure to turn off the automatic drying feature when using this method.

Maintenance Tip

Topping Off and Wiping Down

A simple way to keep the aquarium looking its best between water changes is to keep the water level consistently high enough to hide the waterline. Evaporation is inevitable, so add a few gallons of clean water as soon as a waterline is visible for a consistently tidy appearance.

Depending on how much light the aquarium receives, a slight film of algae may appear on the glass between major maintenances. Keep an algae pad—or, better yet, a magnet-style aquarium glass cleaner—handy to quickly and easily remove incidental algae from the glass. The magnet cleaner can even be kept in the aquarium so that it's always at hand for quick cleanups. Move it to a corner, out of view, when not in use.

↑
These handy magnet algae cleaners make routine removal of algae from the aquarium glass easy. This model even floats, should the two pieces come apart, making it easy to retrieve.

Chapter 6:
Freshwater Live-Planted Aquariums

The freshwater live-planted aquarium possesses, perhaps, the greatest capacity to bring a sense of nature and the look of a natural aquatic setting into the home. A true ecosystem, the interplay between the living plants and the other aquarium inhabitants becomes a point of unmatched fascination and beauty. In the live-planted aquarium, the emphasis is less on the fish than on the aquatic plants, because of their special requirements. There is an old saying among live-planted aquarium hobbyists: "Healthy plants equal healthy fish." This is a proven truth, one that establishes the model by which this aquarium style should be approached.

Before delving too deeply into this most sophisticated style of freshwater aquarium, consider these few points. First, mastery of the live-planted aquarium is not easy; a significant body of knowledge is required for the success and sustainability of a healthy and algae-free aquascape. Second, maintaining a freshwater live-planted aquarium requires patience. You might compare the task to creating a landscape or planting a garden. The garden's lines and direction should be evident from the beginning, but time and effort are necessary for it to grow in and develop the desired shape.

Another concern for those hoping to have a live-planted aquarium custom-installed in their home may be the lack of aquarium maintenance companies or retail fish shops to support the endeavor. This may be more the case in the United States, where saltwater and advanced reef aquariums dominate the high-end market and willing custom installers for live-planted aquariums are hard to find, and less so in Asia and Europe, where, although saltwater aquariums still have the edge, live-planted aquariums are far more popular. Most custom installation and maintenance companies tend to emphasize saltwater aquariums and, to a lesser extent, decorative freshwater aquariums, likely due to ease of operation and greater resource availability.

Fortunately, the Internet and an expanding base of local and regional aquatic plant clubs the world over are serving to expand the knowledge base and provide resources for both information and materials. Regardless, many people find that the freshwater live-planted aquarium remains largely the domain of passionate hobbyists and a select few commercial establishments.

In this chapter, we look at the basics of live-planted aquariums: aesthetic considerations, special equipment and materials, and easy-to-work-with aquatic plants and fish. The Resources section (see page 170) can help steer in the right direction those interested in learning more.

←
A serene freshwater live-planted aquarium brings a natural calm to this simple dining area. This 135-gallon (510 liter) aquarium measures 72 × 18 × 24 inches (183 × 46 × 61 cm).

↓
At 550 gallons (2,081 liters), this freshwater live-planted aquarium is a world unto itself. It may take a year or more for an aquascape like this to really come into form.

The Green Glow: Aesthetics of the Live-Planted Aquarium

A freshwater live-planted aquarium imparts its own special feel to a room. Most are brightly illuminated, with green the dominant color. The many species of aquatic plants contribute various shades of green as well as interesting leaf shapes and textures. Red is also a common primary color among aquatic plants, and red plants in many shades and textures can be found.

Hardscape materials can also have a strong impact on the live-planted aquarium aquascape. Although you can design this aquascape solely with plants, without driftwood or stones, a well-composed hardscape adds dimension to the layout. It can also help hold the general appearance of the composition together during both the start-up phase and the period following major trimming or pruning of the plants. The hardscape components can also be used to harmonize the aquascape with the surrounding space.

Think of the freshwater live-planted aquarium as typically having a softer and more subdued effect in a given room than the average saltwater aquarium. With lots of green, stones, driftwood, and small schooling fish, its look and feel is completely unlike those of saltwater aquariums. Comparisons of freshwater live-planted aquariums and saltwater aquariums are common because their skill level and maintenance requirements are similar, but their aesthetics and visual appeal are very different.

The Glass Box Garden: Aquascaping and Layout Styles

A freshwater live-planted aquarium can be composed in an infinite number of ways. A huge variety of plant species is available, along with many types of stones and driftwood, each with its own unique character. Consider also the nature variable, whereby the natural growth and direction of the plants as they mature create an aquascape that is different but no less beautiful than the intended look. These beautiful accidents defy categorization. To narrow the design focus, choose simple, readily reproducible compositional directions and layouts.

↑
This 75-gallon (284-liter) open-top, live-planted aquarium in a home office expresses absolute compositional simplicity. The homeowner, fond of Japanese aesthetics, wanted an aquascape that embodied some of those qualities. The result uses core elements of only rocks, grass, and fish.

↑
The hardscape is a prominent component of this composition, and in many ways it is the plants that adorn the hardscape, not the other way around. In this space, it is hard to imagine another aquarium style being as well-suited as a freshwater live-planted aquarium.

Zen Simplicity: Minimalist Designs That Work

An interesting approach to aquascaping the live-planted aquarium, the Zen design philosophy involves reducing the compositional elements to their essence. Borrowing from Japanese stone placement techniques and Zen principles of interpreting nature, minimalist layouts emphasize the hardscape material—usually stone—and seek to keep the overall presence of aquatic plants to a bare minimum. Essentially, foliage is used to complement the stone arrangement in the most noncompetitive way possible. The stones play the lead role.

An advantage to this style is that the challenge of growing out and maintaining many species of aquatic plants is eliminated. Time and patience can be focused on the completion of a pleasing stone arrangement that requires only a short grass or groundcover as its accompaniment. Although the system requirements for an aquarium using only groundcover species are similar to those with multiple species and dense planting, managing a few species or a single plant with a specific function in the aquascape is easier. The real benefit is the way in which even a small amount of greenery affects the ambience and appeal of the aquarium.

The Discus Aquarium

Unfortunately, few big aquarium fish are compatible with live plants. This is due largely to either their excessive feeding requirements, which lead to algae problems, or behavioral issues, such as a propensity for digging in the substrate, which can uproot plants. One species, however, is so well-suited to life in the planted aquarium that entire layout styles have evolved around the display of this esteemed fish. The discus (*Symphysodon aequifasciatus*) has been called "the king of the aquarium." Its large ornamental shape and regal demeanor give it a presence unlike that of any other fish in the aquarium. When properly cared for, discus can live for many years in a well-maintained live-planted aquarium.

A discus-specific aquascape calls for two key design considerations. The first has to do with plants. Because discus prefer slightly warmer water temperatures (80–84°F [26–28° C]), and most aquatic plants prefer water that is slightly cooler, or close to room temperature, only plant species that thrive in warmer conditions should be chosen. The hardy *Echinodorus* species (known commonly as sword plant) is an excellent choice. These plants not only tolerate warm water, their large leaves also provide a safe retreat should the fish become frightened. Sword plants also do well in the moderate lighting conditions that discus prefer but that are unsuitable for most live-planted aquariums, which typically require brighter, more intense lighting. (See more on sword plants on page 78.)

↑
These three images show the evolution of a minimalist aquascape. First, the stones are carefully set. The angles of the rocks imbue the layout with tension that is ultimately resolved by the green of the groundcover and the limitation of fish species to just one.

↑
Next, with only the substrate moistened, small bunches (4 to 5 stems each) of the groundcover plant Glossostigma are gently inserted into the substrate with special long tweezers, or pincettes. The tank is then slowly filled with water.

↑
After about six weeks under correct conditions, the finished composition is realized. But this scene won't last forever. As the Glossostigma grows, it becomes deeper and, over time, eventually overgrows the rocks. A layout like this one would likely need to be reworked after about one year. This could involve either just removing the groundcover and replanting or starting over from scratch.

The other key design ingredient for a discus aquarium is the use of a light-colored cosmetic sand or fine gravel in the foreground. This serves multiple purposes. First, it allows a place for food to settle (food doesn't fall between the fine grains and down into the substrate); thus, the discus can graze from the bottom, their preferred feeding method. (Discus actually blow into sand in search of morsels of food.)

Second, fine gravel or sand can be easily vacuumed with a simple gravel-vac siphon device to remove excess food, waste, and debris. Vacuuming also turns over the sand to refresh its pristine appearance. Third, light-colored or white sand encourages the discus to camouflage and thereby show better overall color. Discus normally darken or display dark, vertical stress bars on the sides of their bodies when set against darker gravels and substrates; wild-caught and blue hybrid strains are most notorious for this. Red, orange, and yellow discus hybrids are bred to minimize or eliminate these tendencies.

Healthy Plants = Healthy Fish = Healthy Aquarium: System Design for the Live-Planted Aquarium

The system design for the freshwater live-planted aquarium is generally simple and similar in many respects to that of the decorative freshwater aquarium. One difference, however, is the addition of a system for injecting carbon dioxide (CO_2) into the water column. Through photosynthesis, aquatic plants—just like their terrestrial counterparts—take in CO_2 and give off oxygen. Fish take in oxygen and give off CO_2. In most aquariums, however, the amount of CO_2 produced by the fish and other naturally occurring metabolic activities is insufficient to fully meet the needs of the plants, especially delicate or high-maintenance species. Adding pressurized CO_2 gas at a controlled rate greatly increases the plants' growth rate and vigor. This is not to say

↑
The aquascape of this live-planted aquarium was designed especially for the keeping of discus. The large tank is excellent for maintaining a large group of these revered fish. Aquarium dimensions are 96 × 30 × 30 inches (244 × 76 × 76 cm). Aquarium volume is 375 gallons (1,419 liters).

→
A group of blue diamond discus, a popular hybrid strain, swims lazily about the aquarium. In this layout, the rocks were added for texture and—more important, perhaps—to act as a barrier between the decorative sand and the special substrate in which the plants are growing.

that some plants do not grow without added CO_2, but without question, they grow faster and better with its proper use. The average pressurized CO_2 injection system consists of a carbon dioxide–filled cylinder; an attached regulator, which controls the output of CO_2 into the aquarium; and either a diffuser (which goes inside the aquarium and disperses the CO_2) or a CO_2 reactor (which goes outside the aquarium, usually in line with the canister filter outflow or connected to some means of moving water through the main chamber of the reactor itself). One benefit of the reactor is that it is easily concealed beneath the support stand or cabinetry, allowing one less encumbrance inside the aquarium.

Filtration

Canister filters are, by far, the best choice for the freshwater live-planted aquarium because they can easily be packed with the appropriate filter media for the various stages of plant growth. The key is to choose the right filter size for the given aquarium dimensions, because current and water flow are a concern with this type of aquarium. Too little water flow can contribute to the excessive growth of undesirable anaerobic bacteria in the substrate and to the uneven distribution throughout the aquascape of the CO_2 and nutrients necessary for even and consistent plant growth. Too much current causes many plants to lean over or develop abnormal growth patterns.

Trickle filters can be used, but they can strip CO_2 from the water column and cause the oxidation of essential aquatic plant nutrients before the plants are able to absorb them. A trickle filter designed for live-planted aquariums is required to minimize these effects.

↑
A rock in need of cleaning after several weeks under intense lighting.

↑
A small stainless steel brush purchased from an auto parts store is used to remove the algae growing deep into the surface of the stone.

↑
More of the true color of the rock is exposed. Perched on the rock is an *Otocinculus* catfish, discussed later in this chapter.

Maintenance Tip

Cleaning Rocks

Use a stainless steel or other wire or plastic brush to keep rocks clean. Because of the high-wattage lighting, rocks in the live-planted aquarium may, over time, develop algae, which diminishes their presence in the aquascape. Periodic algae removal with a hard brush restores the necessary contrast the stones provide without getting them so clean that they look unnatural. Some natural algae patina should remain within the fine cracks and pores.

Lighting

In nature, all plants need sunlight for photosynthesis. In the aquarium, the lighting system, which replaces natural sunlight, is one of the essential components for growing plants and keeping them healthy. Either fluorescents or halogen fixtures can be used; the type varies with the layout style and desired species to be maintained. Full-spectrum bulbs designed to light aquatic plants are available in color temperatures from 5,600 K, which emits a yellow to red cast, to 10,000 K, which casts a blue to white light. For the most part, aquatic plants grow under a reasonably wide range of color temperatures, although 6,700 K to 8,500 K offers perhaps the best balance between good growth and pleasing color cast.

In terms of wattage requirements, many competing theories exist. The most widely accepted formula is to use a minimum of 2 watts per gallon (3.8 liters) of water. Wattages from 4 to 6 watts per gallon are not uncommon, although care and close observation are necessary at these intensities to deter or minimize excessive algae growth. These high-wattage systems are probably best used by experienced hobbyists or under the guidance of an aquarium maintenance professional with a background in live-planted aquariums.

From Dawn to Dusk:
The Photoperiod and Day Cycle Simulation
The photoperiod is the most important lighting factor in the freshwater live-planted aquarium. Live-planted aquariums require a sustained period of light of six to ten hours, followed by a period of fourteen to eighteen hours when the lights are off. How long the lights remain on within this range depends on a number of factors. The age of the aquascape is one. When the planted aquarium is newly set up, it may require slightly less light or a shorter photoperiod. As the aquascape matures and the plants become more capable of outcompeting the algae, the duration can be increased. This shorter initial photoperiod approach is especially practical when using intense halogen light sources.

The plant species used can also affect appropriate lighting periods. Some plants thrive under long periods of intense light, while others favor more subdued lighting conditions. Getting the lighting just right can be a tricky task, and experience really comes in handy.

Constant Clarity: Using UV Light
Because of the natural ecological processes occurring in the live-planted aquarium, many of which can produce a cloudy, hazy, or even green water appearance, an ultraviolet (UV) sterilizer light is often employed. This is typically attached to a canister filter or recirculation pump that moves water through the unit and exposes it to UV light, which sterilizes the water and eliminates the cause of the unwanted condition.

A UV sterilizer is particularly useful in larger aquariums—100 gallons (378 liters) or more—in which hazy water conditions are both common and difficult to get rid of, and implementing it before a problem arises is worth considering. In effect, the UV sterilizer keeps the water clear at all times.

←

All live-planted aquariums essentially require the same things: clean water, good lighting, and proper fertilization. This 58-gallon (219 liter) planted aquarium located in an entryway is receiving all three in good measure.

(a)

(b)

(c)

While it does not hurt the aquarium to use a UV sterilizer even if no apparent condition is present, care should be taken not to turn the unit on until the beneficial bacteria are well established and the nitrogen cycle is in full effect. The UV sterilizer does not discriminate and thus kills good bacteria along with the bad, thereby prolonging the time necessary for the aquarium to become chemically stable and ready for fish and other inhabitants. UV lightbulbs have a finite span of effectiveness and typically require annual replacement. Even when they do not yet appear burned out, after a year, their function diminishes or ceases altogether.

Beyond Gravel: Special Substrates for Aquatic Plants

In the freshwater live-planted aquarium, the role of the substrate is far more important than it is in other aquarium styles. Not only should it provide the aquatic plants with needed nutrients, it must also provide a sufficient area for beneficial bacteria to colonize and multiply. For these reasons, special substrates and growing mediums have been developed for planted aquariums. These greatly increase the potential for success and make establishing a healthy planted aquarium that much easier. Though debate about the best growing medium is ongoing (an Internet search on the topic yields a dizzying array of opinions), it is safe to assume that most of the readily available aquatic plant-specific gravels or mediums are better than using plain quartz or other gravel whose purpose is merely aesthetic or decorative.

Maintenance Tip

Bulb Replacement

Lightbulbs diminish in spectrum, brightness, and efficiency as they age. For this reason, replacing bulbs on a live-planted aquarium every six to twelve months is important. Remember that the aquarium light source is the main source of energy for aquatic plants, which require a consistent spectrum and intensity of light for sustained growth and a pleasing appearance. Waiting too long to replace bulbs can result in an abrupt change from a dim to a suddenly bright light source, which can shock the plants and induce a sudden outbreak of algae.

← Flourite from SeaChem (a); Power Sand (b); Aqua Soil Amazonia (c); both from Aqua Design Amano. Power Sand as a top layer, and Aqua Soil as a bottom layer, are designed to be used together.

↗ Only strong, consistent light can grow stemmed plants like these. This 75-gallon (284-liter) aquarium has a single 260-watt power-compact light fixture with a lights-on period of ten consecutive hours per day.

→ Using a UV sterilizer for planted aquariums with discus is a good idea because it keeps the water clear and helps eliminate many pathogens that could infect the fish. Discus require a lot of food, and the waste produced by this heavy feeding often results in water quality issues, a symptom of which is cloudy water.

The Plants

Nature has generously supplied us with a huge selection of attractive and varied aquatic plants—enough, in fact, to warrant huge volumes of books dedicated solely to the categorization and description of species that cover most tropical regions of the world. While the Resources guide on page 170 lists excellent resources for delving into the hundreds of plant types commonly kept in aquariums, this section only touches on the main groups and those of particular interest from an aquascaping perspective—in other words, plants that are more readily available, easier to keep, and that serve a specific aesthetic or compositional function.

Anubias nana

One of the easiest of all aquatic plants to grow is the hardy and versatile *Anubias nana* (also called *Anubias barteri* var. nana). This charming little plant is one of the most common plants used by both beginners and experienced hobbyists. Aquarium design and maintenance companies are fond of it, too, for its reliability and flexible aquascaping potential.

Anubias nana is among the handful of plants that actually grow (and, some say, do better) attached to a stone, piece of driftwood, or hardscape element rather than planted in the substrate. Its dark green, rotund leaves are distinctive, forming an effective contrast to the many plants with which it might share a composition.

↑
Generally categorized as a low-light plant, *Anubias nana* tolerates a wide range of water and lighting conditions.

Ferns

All of the commonly available fern species are excellent long-term, low-maintenance plants. Generally classified as shade plants, aquatic ferns do well in low and moderate lighting conditions, and they even do well placed in areas that receive little light—under a large branch of driftwood, for example, or beneath taller plants whose leaves drape over the water surface.

Aquatic ferns grow better when attached to driftwood or stones than when planted in the substrate, so a special growing medium or gravel is not necessary. In fact, it is possible to create a lovely aquascape solely from attached species of plants. For these, any decorative gravel or cosmetic sand suffices as a substrate.

Mosses

Mosses play a special role in the aquascape. They can soften hard surfaces such as driftwood and stone and serve as added texture. Their presence suggests the idyllic aquatic environment we might imagine existing in nature.

Java moss is by far the most popular, versatile, and readily available type of moss. When it grows too thick, it can be thinned by gently pulling it or by using trimming scissors. Unlike most other aquatic plants, which float when trimmed, mosses sink, so be sure to remove the trimmings right away. Even a few stray clippings can become a nuisance if they are allowed to grow into other sections of the aquascape.

Most mosses prefer slightly cooler water (72–75°F [22–25°C]). In water that is too warm due to excessive heat from lights and poor ventilation or an unusually warm room temperature, mosses are among the first plants to show signs of distress by curling or looking dry.

←
This freshwater live-planted aquarium is an open-top style that features many species of stemmed plants in the background which require frequent trimming. The root bound and attached species, which comprise the midground, require only periodic thinning—usually just a few leaves at a time. The foreground is a delicate green carpeting plant that spreads by runners. It, too, requires only periodic thinning.

↑
Narrow-leaf Java fern is an aquascaping favorite for its long, thin leaves. It forms a wonderful contrast to plants like *Anubias nana*.

↑
Java moss is used here as a groundcover. It is attached to stones with green cotton thread and placed along the foreground of the aquascape, where it slowly grows in.

↑
Here, Java moss that was tied to driftwood with cotton thread has become attached to the wood.

←
This freshwater live-planted aquarium uses both stemmed plants (center), which require frequent trimming, and root-bound plants (along the background), which require only periodic thinning—usually just a few blades or leaves at a time. The darker plant in the midground is a species of *Crytocoryne*.

Sword Plants

Bold and beautiful, the sword plant, or *Echinodorus*, is among the most popular and easily grown ornamental plants. The classic Amazon sword (*Echinodorus blehri*) can be found in almost any retail aquarium shop offering live aquatic plants. Its broad leaves and lovely green color, combined with its tolerance of a wide range of lighting and other aquarium conditions, help this plant find its way into many lovely aquascapes.

There are enough leaf shapes, colors, and textures among the various species of *Echindorus* to create compositions solely of sword plants. Most varieties grow quite large under good conditions, however, so swords require a large aquarium—75 gallons (284 liters)—to reach their full glory and potential. *Echinodorus uraguayensis* may produce 100 or more long, slender leaves from a single specimen at one time. An attractive hybrid such as *Echinodorus* 'ozelot' offers a nice size contrast to the larger species, as it tends to stay smaller. All of the sword plants, however, make excellent background plants—filling in and establishing the foundation of a good aquascape.

A nutritious substrate is a must for these heavy root feeders. Although adding CO_2 to the aquarium can help sword plants grow larger and healthier, they do quite well in established aquariums in which CO_2 is not used.

Cryptocorynes

Another aquatic plant group whose members do well in aquariums without CO_2 injection and under varying lighting conditions are the *Cryptocorynes*, or crypts for short. Like all aquatic plants, however, crypts do better in the long term in an aquarium with added CO_2. While many crypts are fussy when first planted, once they are well established, they can thrive for long periods with proper care.

It is not uncommon, from time to time, for the leaves on these plants to appear to be melting, often after a sudden change in water conditions. In most cases, this condition is temporary; once the aquarium stabilizes, new leaves generally appear.

Categorized typically as a shade plant, *Cryptocorynes* is a good choice for planting in areas of the aquascape that do not receive much direct light—under an overhanging piece of driftwood or taller sword plants, for example. Crypts can serve as a sharp contrast to brighter, taller light-requiring species, playing the

↑
The Amazon sword: for years, an easy-to-grow favorite.

↑
A nice group of bronze crypts helps fill the midground of this aquascape.

role of the shadow or dark element in the composition. It is also possible to compose a layout made solely of *Cryptocorynes* species, as there are many heights, colors, and shapes of plants from which to choose, and most have the same basic requirements. Foreground, midground, and background can all be sufficiently occupied by different *Cryptocorynes*.

Stemmed Plants

Of the major aquatic plant groups, stemmed plants boast more members with more varying characteristics than perhaps any other. Individual stems of the same species are usually planted in groups or bunches. With time and frequent trimming, even a small bunch can grow into a thriving section of an aquascape, bringing a refreshing burst of color to the composition.

Many stemmed plant species can be likened to flowers in a landscape—providing the color and focal point to the layout—while others serve more as hedges—filling in open areas and offering sculptability through a regimen of frequent trimming. Most species require CO_2 and strong lighting (at least 2 watts per gallon [3.8 liters]), especially if a dense stand of lush growth is desired.

Stemmed plants require higher maintenance than the groups previously discussed, and trimming techniques often require time and experience to master.

Groundcovers

Few plant groups can contribute depth and sophistication to a live-planted aquarium composition like the groundcovers. These plants stay short, grow densely in the foreground, and can occasionally be used else where in specific layout styles. The skillful application of groundcovers gives an aquascape an idyllic charm that is difficult to obtain without them. All the popular species require CO_2 injection and strong lighting to grow properly (or at all).

The only downside to groundcovers is that most require frequent and precise trimming. Even then, most eventually grow too thickly, growing over and on top of themselves until the bottommost layers become leggy as they are starved of light and nutrients. Fortunately, most groundcovers can be fairly easily removed by gently lifting whole sections from the substrate. The shallow root systems do not usually create much mess, and the best plants from the top sections may be replanted and enjoyed again and again.

↑
Stemmed plants are some of the most beautiful, colorful, and exotic of all aquarium plants. Many species can be used like flowers in the aquascape.

The Fish

Clearly, plant health and a high level of presentation are paramount to creating a beautiful and effective aquascape in the freshwater live-planted aquarium. But what is an aquarium without attractive fish?

The need to provide foremost for the well-being of the plants limits the types—and potentially the number—of fish that can be kept long term in the freshwater live-planted aquarium. Most of those reviewed in the chapter on decorative freshwater aquariums are unsuitable for a live-planted aquarium, largely because the aquatic plants are a favorite menu item for those fish! Here is an introduction to the fish types known to coexist peacefully with aquatic plants.

Tetras

By far, the best fish choice for live-planted aquariums is tetras. While a few members of the tetra family are incompatible with planted aquariums, they are substantially outnumbered by those that are. In fact, some of the most brightly colored tetras thrive only in aquariums with exceptional water quality and conditions such as those necessary for sustaining healthy aquatic plants. Most live-planted aquarium systems achieve many of the key water parameters found in the vast Amazon and Rio Negro regions of South America, where most tetras are collected. Their unusually bright colors, which provide so much visual interest to planted aquariums, are likely an adaptive trait resulting from the dark, murky waters of these rivers. The fishes' intense colors help them find one another under conditions of low visibility.

↗
A swirl of beautiful fish in a large live-planted aquarium.

↗
Glo-lite tetras, so named for their iridescent pink stripe, which appears to glow.

→
With their intense blue and red coloration, this school of cardinal tetras completes a scene of primary colors.

Tetras in the wild are typically schooling fish, clustering for all sorts of survival reasons. In the aquarium, the extent to which they school depends on several factors. Some species are simply more prone to school than others and seem to stay together in unified groups no matter the situation, while others tend to scatter, each unto itself, unless suddenly frightened or threatened. Often, the presence of other species or perhaps a small group of a larger fish is required to convince tetras to school.

Neons and Cardinals
Most people are familiar with the classic neon tetra (*Paracheirodon innesi*). With its brilliant blue and red lines, the neon tetra is one of the most striking of the commonly available little freshwater fish. Many people, however, may not be as familiar with the neon tetra's even more stunning cousin, the cardinal tetra (*Paracheirodon axelrodi*).

Cardinal tetras tend to grow slightly larger than neons and have far more red coloration. They are often mistakenly referred to as neons, so being aware of the difference can help ensure you get the desired fish for your aquarium. In some layouts, the bold red of the cardinal may be a bit too much color, and the slightly more subdued red of neons is a better fit. In other layouts, the striking contrast of the red cardinal against the deep green of the aquatic plants draws attention to the fish.

A third and slightly less common relative of the neon and cardinal tetra is the green neon, or simulans tetra, also called the false neon tetra (*Paracheirodon simulans*). This fish sports the same blue line as the other two, but far less red. Just how much red the fish shows varies with different aquascapes, lighting conditions, and other factors. It is not uncommon for simulans tetras to show no detectable red coloration at all.

Rummy-Nose Tetras
Another attractive favorite for the freshwater live-planted aquarium is the rummy-nose tetra. Unlike the neons and cardinals, which tend to scatter, rummy-nose tetras are excellent schooling fish that almost always stay in a tight group—a pleasing effect. The rummy-nose's rather plain silvery body gives way to a gorgeous, deep-red head and a black and white, almost checkerboard-patterned tail. The rummy-nose tetra harmonizes with virtually any aquascape containing live plants.

The Congo Tetra
Native to the Congo River in western Africa, the Congo tetra is one of the handful of larger tetras that do well in a densely planted freshwater aquarium. Male Congo tetras' broad bodies

↗
Rummy-nose tetras (center) swim in a tetra paradise with their tankmates—blood-fin tetras and long-finned Congo tetras.

→
Congo tetras (center) seek cover under some plants. These three are males, which are much more colorful than females. Many retail fish stores don't even offer female Congo tetras because the males, with their good coloration and long fins, are what most people want.

reveal a powdery blue and yellow iridescence, and they develop long, flowing fins as they mature. With their large size and peaceful temperament, they add a lovely dimension to the fish selection of a live-planted aquarium.

Angelfish

Discussed in chapter 5 as a tropical fish suitable for the decorative freshwater aquarium, angelfish are also a popular choice for live-planted aquariums. The naturally softer water and more acidic conditions of planted aquariums are ideal for angelfish, and they are among the relatively few species of larger ornamental fish suitable for planted aquariums. Their vertical lines and exquisite features suit a sophisticated composition of aquatic plants.

Cleaning Machines: Algae-eaters for the Live-Planted Aquarium

With their high-wattage lighting and CO_2 injection, freshwater live-planted aquariums grow not only lovely plants but also grow not-so-lovely algae. Fortunately, a few animals are tremendously helpful in controlling the incidental algae that grows every day in a planted aquarium. They are especially valuable in the early stages of a live-planted aquarium, when plants are still in fierce competition with algae for the upper hand in terms of growth and nutrient absorption.

Algae-Eating Shrimp
Popularized for use in aquariums by renowned Japanese master aquarium artist Takashi Amano, the algae-eating shrimp (*Caridinia japonica*, also called Amano shrimp) is one of the best algae-eaters or scavengers available for live-planted aquariums. Constantly eating, these little shrimp are a lot of fun to watch, but they are too small and unobtrusive to get in the way of the aquascape. In fact, they blend right in to the point where it's

↗
A true wild-form angelfish. This one comes from Peru.

→
Caridinia japonica, or Algae-eating shrimp, are native to Japan, but now available all over the world.

possible to forget they are in the aquarium at all! The shrimp will snack on a very few species of soft-leafed plants, but, for the most part, they are safe and can be found in almost all live-planted aquariums.

O-Cats: Otocinculus Catfish

This tiny dwarf suckermouth fish plays a similar role to the Plecostomus discussed in chapter 5. The Otocinculus catfish, or O-cat, for short, uses its specially designed mouth to lightly graze softer algae from plants, rocks, driftwood, and even the aquarium glass. This fish is especially effective against the soft, powdery brown algae common in most newly set-up aquariums.

Algae Eating Sharks

Algae-eating sharks, often called Siamese algae eaters, are terrific allies in the war against daily algae. Attractive and amusing in small groups, these fish eat the persistent algae not eaten by shrimp and O-cats. Algae-eating sharks are peaceful and compatible with most fish suitable for a live-planted aquarium. They can, however, grow fairly large—possibly in excess of 5 inches (13 cm). Fortunately, these sharks are usually sold as small juveniles and may enjoy a long time in even a small aquarium of 20 to 30 gallons (76 to 114 liters) before growing too large.

Nerite Snails

About the size of a thumbnail, nerite snails are most effective for cleaning algae from hardscape materials, such as rocks or driftwood, in the aquarium. There is no type of algae that nerite snails do not devour with remarkable speed. It is not uncommon for a large group of twenty or more to completely clean whole large rocks or pieces of wood in a matter of days. A half-dozen or so added to nearly any planted aquarium in the first few weeks goes a long way toward ensuring a clean and algae-free hardscape.

↑
Together with the algae-eating shrimp, O-cats help keep in check the day-to-day algae that grows in planted aquariums.

↑
Long, brownish shark-shaped algae eaters are peaceful and compatible.

↑
Unlike other snails, nerites do not reproduce in the aquarium, so overpopulation is not a problem.

Design Tip

Avoiding a Fish Circus

Avoid mixing too many species in the same aquarium, particularly when working with groups of small fish, such as tetras, and when a calming schooling effect is desired. When more than two or three groups of twelve or more individuals are used, the fish tend to scatter and mix throughout the aquarium, creating a jumbled scene with few or no coherent groups.

Maintenance and
Long-Term Considerations
for the Live-Planted Aquarium

The freshwater live-planted aquarium brings unmatched beauty and sophistication to nearly any interior space, but to keep it looking like a work of aquatic art requires a considerable amount of maintenance and operator input. Because it is always growing and changing, it is highly probable that the day will come when the aquascape outgrows any real sense of composition and must be reworked or taken out and redesigned. Following are maintenance basics (in no way a complete guide to planted aquarium maintenance) and a guide to recognizing when it is time to rework the aquascape or start over altogether.

The Underwater Gardener:
Planted Aquarium Maintenance Basics

Incorporating a freshwater live-planted aquarium in the home is an attractive idea; from a design standpoint, it may be the perfect complement for a particular room. But core maintenance requirements must be followed for a live-planted aquarium to come into form and retain and express the beauty that made it such an attractive option in the first place. Theories and approaches to the many planted aquarium maintenance variables abound. This book is designed to give you a feel for what's involved and will help you decide whether the live-planted aquarium style is worth exploring, given your desire, time, and budget. We begin with the most fundamental task in the maintenance of any aquarium: the water change.

Water Changes

As a matter of routine, a live-planted aquarium requires a weekly water change of 30 to 50 percent regardless of layout, plants, or livestock levels. While some layout styles and plant selections can move this requirement closer to biweekly, this is likely not possible until the aquarium is stable and conditions are well balanced (plants are growing nicely, water is clear, fish look healthy), which seldom occurs in fewer than two months. Even if a less intensive water change schedule proves acceptable, an algae film may appear on the glass after a few days or a week, and many aquariums lose enough water to evaporation that they must be topped off before the next water change.

The main benefit to frequent small water changes can be summed up in two words: algae control. Consistently replacing one-third to one-half of the aquarium water removes many of the variables that lead to algae outbreaks. And remember—the use of strong lighting and CO_2 injection creates prime conditions not just for aquatic plant growth but for algae, as well.

In most areas, tap water is fine for water changes, as long as chlorine is removed. Liquid dechlorinators or special activated carbon–filled filtration bottles attached to the faucet or water supply work well. The latter is perhaps the easier and more reliable method; professional maintenance companies often use this approach to dechlorinating tap water. (Not all cities, regions, or countries add chlorine, so verify this first if you're unsure about your water source.)

Trimming and Pruning the Plants

As long as their basic needs are consistently provided for, aquatic plants are always growing. You must study the techniques, knowledge, experience, and overall expertise required for trimming and maintaining the plants if a live-planted aquarium

↑

The aquascape of this 40-gallon (151-liter) live-planted aquarium is designed for long-term sustainability. At the time this photo was taken, the aquascape was already two years old and still going strong. The open foreground and use of mostly *Anubias nana* and ferns make routine maintenance and pruning easy.

←

This 58-gallon (219-liter) live-planted aquarium has a little bit of everything: stemmed plants, moss, ferns, and *Anubias*. The open foreground adds depth, and the symmetrical composition makes obvious the reference points for trimming the plants. Symmetrical compositions are especially useful for beginners and those new to freshwater-planted aquariums who lack experience with trimming and more advanced layout styles.

is what you seek. If you plan to have a maintenance company manage the aquarium, be sure the staff members possess the necessary skills to properly shape and maintain the plants over the life of your layout.

With so many potential plant combinations and accompanying trimming and pruning requirements, it is probably easiest to simply state that most aquatic plants require some form of growth control through the physical removal of leaves and stems on the order of two to three times per month. Trimming detail is likely necessary at each water change; only the amount of plant material needing attention varies, with some weeks needing a lot, other weeks needing but a snip or two here and there. Seldom, if ever, does an aquascape not need ongoing growth management to maintain the integrity of the composition.

Fertilization

Another subject that engenders tremendous discussion and competing philosophies is the fertilization of aquatic plants. Fortunately, most approaches are just slightly different versions of the same general concepts. For the sake of brevity, the subject can be reduced to this statement: Aquatic plants require the regular addition of liquid fertilizers and nutrients to the water. This generally takes place just after the water change but may also be required at intervals between water changes. Typically, fertilization regimens include iron, potassium, micronutrients such as magnesium and boron, and, in some systems, the macronutrients nitrogen and phosphorus. Fortunately, forms made specifically for aquarium use are commonly available through tropical fish stores and online retailers.

All Good Things Must End: Long-Term Considerations

It is an inescapable reality of life, and certainly of the freshwater live-planted aquarium: There comes a point when the aquarium's composition no longer provides the desired scenery. Due simply to the passage of time and the growth of the plants beyond the point of recovery, a live-planted aquarium eventually must be started over. The exact point in the aquarium's lifespan at which this occurs is impossible to predict, but, on average, two to three years is considered a long run for any layout. While some may go on longer—five years is not unheard of—such life spans should not be expected but, rather, taken as a fortunate surprise. Without question, through appropriate planning in the beginning, an aquascape that lasts many years is achievable. It pays to do thorough research or find a qualified installation and maintenance professional before proceeding.

Reworking the Layout

Short of completely starting over, most live-planted aquariums can simply be reworked, just as we might replant flower beds in our home landscaping in the spring or, leaving the essential lines intact, create a new look by planting new shrubs. The same is possible with a viable but overgrown live-planted aquarium. The process can be messy and time-consuming, but it is doable. Success comes down to examining all the factors—time, budget, materials, objectives—for the aquarium within the space. Many people are ready for a new look after a few years, and starting over is within their budget. Others may have a great hardscape in good condition that just needs fresh flora to revitalize it.

The important thing to remember is the ephemeral nature of most live-planted aquarium layouts. A beautiful composition may remain that way for a short time only, so the eventual decision to rework or replace is fundamental to live-planted aquarium ownership. With that in mind, the appropriateness of this challenging aquarium style for your space may be accurately assessed.

↑
Although its aquascape is simple, this 70-gallon (265-liter) bowfront aquarium requires a high level of maintenance. The grass (*Lilaeopsis*) in the foreground and the *Glossostigma* forming the green mounds in the back must be pruned and trimmed weekly to keep the layout from getting out of control.

←
This 550-gallon (2,081-liter) densely planted aquarium is designed for long-term sustainability and makes excellent use of Anubias, ferns, and *Cryptocoryne* species.

Part 03: Saltwater Aquariums

↑
A spectacular 540-gallon (2,043-liter) decorative saltwater aquarium captures the essence of this aquarium style with an excellent selection of fish and beautifully composed coral arrangement, plus the distinctive touch of the black onyx substrate.

It is hard to deny the impact of a saltwater aquarium. The exotic and intensely colorful fish and corals, coupled with a deep blue light spectrum, form a luminous and almost otherworldly scene rich in pattern and detail.

If we have a narrow sense of what a saltwater aquarium should look like, it is because we have a defined vision of what the ocean environment looks like; the aesthetics and design expression are self-evident. We are also familiar with many of the best fish and other animals for saltwater aquariums, and their ready availability means we see those same species used frequently. In fact, their popularity and familiarity is evident even in pop culture—the blockbuster movie *Finding Nemo*, in which all the main characters were true-to-form depictions of commonly kept saltwater aquarium fish, is a prime example.

We are much more familiar with the classic decorative saltwater aquarium and even the live coral reef aquarium than we are with freshwater aquariums. This is due, in part, to the greater presence of these saltwater aquarium styles in public places, such as restaurants and office waiting rooms, and also in private residences with custom-designed and professionally maintained aquariums. They are always popular and, when properly executed, create a visually stunning and sophisticated aquatic canvas that enlivens rooms with the wondrous beauty of the ocean.

↑
This 375-gallon (1,419-liter) live coral reef aquarium represents the pinnacle of aquarium keeping.

Chapter 7: Decorative Saltwater Aquariums

When many of us think of a beautiful, professionally-installed custom aquarium, we think of the decorative saltwater style. This style has long been emphasized by professional aquarium installation and maintenance companies, who take advantage of the instant impact provided by the amazing and colorful fish. It is no wonder many of them choose to focus solely on this most impressive aquarium style.

The composition of a decorative saltwater aquarium consists of two primary elements: skeletal coral, either natural or fabricated, and fish, which are, of course, the real focal point. The primary substrate is almost always some form of crushed coral or sand, which is available in virtually every imaginable size and shade. The decorative saltwater aquarium requires more specialized equipment than freshwater installations, the need for which becomes clear when one considers that almost every marine aquarium fish available today is collected from the ocean. They are, in effect, wild animals whose dynamic natural environment provides specific conditions and foods. So the goal of the decorative saltwater aquarium is to simulate at least the general conditions found in the primarily tropical regions in which the fish are collected. Supporting the long-term health of these fish requires a more sophisticated system than that needed for almost any freshwater aquarium. Fortunately, practical experience and today's technology have converged to yield the knowledge and technical ability to keep these beautiful animals in home aquariums.

While a significant part of this chapter is about creating an aquascape for your saltwater aquarium that harmonizes with your space, the overall emphasis is on fish selection and system requirements, simply because the design elements available for decorative saltwater aquariums are limited.

←
This aquarium, with its classic, decorative saltwater layout style, works in a wide array of decors.

The Ocean Aesthetic: The Impact of the Decorative Saltwater Aquarium

Though the fundamental design and aquascaping components are consistent among layouts, decorative saltwater aquariums can integrate well into just about any interior design style. While the principal aesthetic of the decorative saltwater aquarium suggests an abstract or contemporary design sense, the regal and refined appearance of many marine aquarium fish certainly make this style compatible with traditional or classical décor as well. As with any aquarium style, the key to creating a successful aquascape is to look for fish and other design elements that fulfill your personal design sensibilities.

The impact of a decorative saltwater aquarium on a room is usually striking. The interesting shapes, patterns, and colors of the large ornamental fish set against a theater of beautiful decorative coral makes a strong design statement and establishes immediate visual interest. This style's powerful, almost iconic, reference to the ocean is at once intriguing and nostalgic. The fish provide a subject for great conversation, and the many fascinating characters that inhabit a marine fish aquarium are sure to garner the attention of guests. Although it is possible to create a more subdued aquascape, subtlety of design is probably best left to the freshwater aquarium.

Variations on a Theme: Layout Concepts and Materials for the Decorative Saltwater Aquarium

If it seems that the potential compositional elements for a decorative saltwater aquarium are limited, it's because—well, they are! There are a few reasons for this, not the least of which is that many of the rocks and decorative elements we would use in a freshwater aquarium simply do not last in saltwater. Many types of rock react unfavorably and cause water quality issues, while other just disintegrate over time. Fortunately, materials for creating an effective and attractive setting are readily available. Skeletal corals of varying form and texture form the foundation.

Skeletal Coral from Ocean Reefs

The natural coral we commonly see decorating saltwater aquariums is actually the hard skeletal remains of a once-thriving colony of living creatures. For many years, it was the only decorative material used to aquascape a saltwater aquarium. But natural skeletal coral has since fallen out of favor for a number of reasons.

One is that most types of natural skeletal coral are extremely brittle, and keeping high-quality pieces from chipping and breaking during collection, transport, and distribution is difficult and costly. Another concern is the environmental impact of removing skeletal coral from reefs. Collection practices have become highly regulated; much less is collected, and what is collected is expensive. For these reasons, this book emphasizes fabricated and cast-molded coral and the many advantages of using it.

←
This home office is enlivened by the natural touch of a custom built-in marine aquarium instead of more bookshelves or storage behind the desk.

→
Lace rock adds a natural feel to an intricate composition that includes mostly cast-molded coral with some natural skeletal coral.

←
Examples of natural skeletal coral

Improving on Nature: Cast-Molded Coral

Cast-molded coral has, without question, become a staple for aquascaping the decorative saltwater aquarium. It provides much the same beauty and elegance as real skeletal coral, but at a substantially lower cost and without harming natural reef environments. In fact, in the absence of a keen eye for such things, most people assume it is the real thing.

But the benefits of cast-molded coral don't end there. From an aquascaping standpoint, it is much easier to work with due to its level base. As part of the production process, the coral pieces are given a flat bottom so they stand straight and level and can be more easily arranged into the desired composition. The inherent irregularities of natural coral often made it difficult or impossible to fit individual pieces into the layout in the desired way. This usually resulted in compromising the intended design to some extent. Another advantage of cast-molded coral is that pieces of the same or similar size can be easily acquired, which makes composing the decorative saltwater aquascape easier.

Cast-molded coral is also more durable. Made from nontoxic polymers, it is far less brittle than the real thing, and many surface details of natural coral can be modified in the molding and production processes, which greatly reduces the potential for chips and breakage.

Design Tip

Simple Themed Designs with Decorative Coral

To create a simple, uncluttered backdrop for the fish, limit the types or varieties of decorative coral you use. A simple background keeps the shapes and color patterns of the fish from being lost in a busy, decorative coral arrangement. For example, use several large blue pieces, with only one or two contrasting pieces for effect.

↑
Because cast-molded coral can be easily and consistently packaged, new pieces always arrive in near-perfect condition, free of the storage and transport damage inflicted on natural skeletal coral.

↑
Volcanic rock can usually be found at landscape supply stores and rock yards. Be sure to rinse it thoroughly before using it in the aquarium.

↑
In this 300-gallon (1,135-liter) bowfront display, pieces of live rock conceal the lines between the decorative coral and the crushed coral substrate, which is kept thin for easy cleaning.

Accent and Texture: Rocks for Decorative Saltwater Aquariums

The rocks you might use in a freshwater aquarium are unsuitable for a saltwater aquarium because they can adversely affect the water chemistry and cause a host of problems for the aquarium inhabitants. However, some types of rock are just fine for use in a decorative saltwater aquarium, and they can play a valuable role in the seamless integration of cast-molded coral into the aquascape.

Volcanic and Lace Rock

Most rocks of volcanic origin are safe to use in saltwater aquariums, as are similar rocks categorized as lace rock. These rocks, which are available in several colors and textures, can relieve the monotony of the decorative coral and are great for breaking the line created by the coral's flat base. The textural contrast between the rocks and the coral can also be effective.

Some aquarium professionals suggest that lace rock may cause water chemistry and quality problems in saltwater aquariums. No conclusion has been reached, but it makes sense to consider all the variables when planning any aquarium. It should be noted that some of the saltwater aquariums featured in this book use lace rock without negative results.

Live Rock

Live rock consists of rock pieces and fragments collected from natural ocean reefs. Its primary application in live coral reef aquariums is to form the base structure for the live corals and other invertebrates. In the decorative saltwater aquarium, it is often used like lava and lace rock: to add texture and help break lines between decorative coral compositions.

Live rock also has the potential to introduce to the aquarium additional beneficial bacteria, which help process fish waste and food, and that is always good. But this occurs only if the live rock is fresh and has undergone proper transport and handling—not exposed to extreme temperatures for extended periods, for instance. Otherwise, the many beneficial microbes that give live rock its name may be lost.

Substrates for Decorative Saltwater Aquariums

Most substrates used for saltwater aquariums possess valuable buffering properties that help stabilize and maintain the pH of the aquarium water. Decorative and artificially colored quartz gravels and other substrates made for use in freshwater aquariums not only lack this beneficial buffering capacity but also may react unfavorably with saltwater, losing their dyes and shiny coating.

↑
Ornamental saltwater fish form a swirl of color around a decorative coral centerpiece.

The substrate or bottom cover for the decorative saltwater aquarium can have a profound effect on the overall appearance of the aquascape. With fewer total design elements to work with in this aquarium style, substrates are a valuable asset in the pursuit of a harmonious composition.

Crushed Coral

The most commonly used substrate for decorative saltwater aquariums is crushed coral. It is available in many grades, sizes, and colors, although these are mostly shades of cream, white, and pink. The size range runs from fine sand to large fragments, with mixtures both homogeneous and disparate. However, while crushed coral is safe—it has no adverse affect on water chemistry—it does have disadvantages. The fine, sandlike grades of crushed coral can be problematic in high-circulation aquariums. If the current created by a filter outflow or recirculation pump is too strong, it can blow the sand particles around too much. This not only causes bare spots to appear on the aquarium bottom, but the sand can be sucked into the filter intake, where it can cause grinding or even the failure of vital moving parts inside the motor. Large fish quickly darting away from the bottom of the aquarium can also stir up the fine sands in much the same manner.

Aragonite

Aragonite is a calcium carbonate mineral that makes a superb substrate medium for saltwater aquariums. Like crushed coral, it provides excellent buffering capacity; it also contributes useful trace elements to the water. As well, it helps reduce the water's nitrate content, which is beneficial for the fish and for controlling algae growth. It, too, comes in various granule sizes, though the selection is more limited than for crushed coral. Aragonite is often the preferred choice of aquarium installation and maintenance companies.

Maintenance Tip

For Easy Cleaning, Keep It Thin

Keeping the substrate in a decorative saltwater aquarium in a thin layer—just enough to cover the bottom—makes cleaning much easier. There's no real advantage to greater substrate depth, anyway, unless you have one of the few types of fish that like to burrow into the substrate at night or when frightened. Use a gravel vacuum siphon to clean the substrate bottom at least once per month. You can even siphon it all out, rinse it with clean water, and replace it.

Primary Colors

Take advantage of the decorative saltwater aquarium's bold colors. Strong, deep blues, brilliant reds, and perfect greens can provide any space with a dash of living color and a strong design focal point.

The Fish

The real stars of the decorative saltwater aquarium, are, of course, the fish. With their vast and varied representation of nature's art in motion, these jewels of the sea present many high-impact design opportunities. Their beauty and exoticism have kept decorative saltwater aquariums at the forefront of aquarium design for many years. With the right understanding of the characteristics and needs of ornamental saltwater fish, it is possible to create aquarium designs of diverse form and color with inimitable style.

A Cast of Characters: The Many Faces of Saltwater Aquarium Fish

Saltwater fish commonly collected for the aquarium trade are found on reefs. Reef fishes are far more colorful and varied than open-water marine fish, which makes them the obvious candidates for display in home aquariums. The dynamism of the reef environment has produced several distinct groups of fish, whose members have similar general characteristics, but unique patterns and features. In the following section, we look at the main groups of commonly available fish and get a feel for their behaviors, needs, and influences on decorative saltwater aquascapes.

Angelfish
Not to be confused with freshwater angelfish, marine angelfish are among the loveliest and most impressive saltwater fish available. They are often available as juveniles, some of which show entirely different, but no less striking, coloration patterns than their adult forms. In contrast to their namesake, however, angelfish can be a bit pugnacious and generally hold their own with larger, even more aggressive fish.

To keep these fish successfully requires superb water quality. They are omnivorous, and they tend to do well on high-quality prepared frozen fish food. Popular species include the queen angelfish, blue-ring or *Annularis* angelfish, French angelfish, and the iconic emperor angelfish.

Triggers
These fish, with their oval bodies and small, toothy mouths, are among the hardiest of ornamental saltwater aquarium fish. Temperaments range dramatically from very aggressive to reasonably peaceful, with the more popular and readily available species tending toward the latter. Even these, however, are known to be amiable at first, only to turn mean after several months. Their diet consists of mostly meaty foods, and some may even be handfed—though cautiously, as their jaws are quite powerful! Popular species include the Huma-Huma or Picasso trigger (whose coloration pattern could be mistaken for a work of abstract art), the Niger trigger, and the clown trigger.

Tangs
A popular and exceedingly beautiful group of saltwater fish, tangs can be found in just about every well-stocked decorative saltwater aquarium. Though they can be aggressive toward one another, they are generally compatible with most other similarly sized fish, despite occasional bossiness. Yellow and blue species are the most often used for their intense primary colorations, but a wide range of color patterns exists. Diets must include algae or green-based foods. Popular, hardy tang species include the powder-blue, Pacific blue, yellow, Sohal, and Naso.

↓
A stunning blue-face angelfish

↓
The queen of them all, the queen angelfish

↑
A rare blamengi tang

↑
The clown trigger—a hardy and vivacious character indeed. The clown trigger's mellow coloration distinguishes it among more brightly colored tankmates.

↓
The yellow tang remains a staple of available saltwater fish.

Wrasses

Wrasses are adored for their comical swimming patterns; many burrow in the substrate at night or when frightened. Several of the large wrasses are staples of the decorative saltwater aquarium. Their elongated body shapes add contrast to the predominantly oval and rounded shapes of the other common species in the aquarium. Wrasses are highly compatible with most other popular fish groups and do well on a meaty diet of high-quality frozen foods. Popular species for decorative saltwater aquariums include the harlequin tusk, green-bird wrasse, and lunar wrasse.

Puffers

Everybody loves a puffer! The puffer's animated and expressive face reveals an intelligence of sorts that people respond and even get attached to. While they do have interesting and colorful patterns, they are most sought after for their characteristic chubby shape and mild temperament—though they can be aggressive toward one another when more than one is kept in the same aquarium.

Puffers are not likely to puff up often in the aquarium. This defense strategy is usually employed in the face of a significant threat. Puffers enjoy a varied diet, with an occasional feeding of fresh shellfish. Popular species include the dogface, spiny, Sapo, and golden puffers.

Lionfish

The majestic lionfish is a classic favorite for the decorative saltwater aquarium. One of the hardiest species commonly kept, lionfish are well known for their poisonous dorsal spines.

Be careful to avoid bumping or touching these fish when working in the aquarium. Look for individuals weaned onto meaty prepared foods and freeze-dried krill (a type of crustacean), because lionfish initially want to eat live foods only, and weaning can take some time. Once on the prepared foods, however, they are easy to feed and care for, although they still eat any tankmate small enough to fit in their mouth. The Volitans lionfish is far and away the most commonly kept species, and not many other species share its widespread availability.

Damselfishes

Most damsels are as hardy as they are pugnacious—two characteristics they seem to possess in spades. They are, in fact, so well known for their hardiness that they are almost always the first fish to be added to a saltwater aquarium, their role being to start the nitrogen cycle (see page 35). Due to their small size, they do stand to be eaten if larger ornamental fish are the primary aquarium inhabitants—especially predators such as the popular Volitans lionfish. However, if a large enough group of damsels is present, a few of the toughest almost always survive and go on to stake claims to a favorite territory, which they fiercely defend.

These stubborn little fish add dimension to the fish selection because they are a good deal smaller than the others; they are, however, no less capable of holding their own when confronted!

Damsels eat just about any prepared marine fish food. Popular species include green chromis, yellowtail blue damsels, and striped damsels.

↓
The comical and fast-swimming harlequin tusk

↓
The sapo puffer

↓
The golden puffer's bright yellow color makes it a focal point in the composition. The puffer's unique shape and facial features contribute strongly to the otherworldly notions we harbor about marine fish.

↑
The *Volitans* lionfish is far and away the most commonly kept lionfish species; not many other species share its widespread availability.

Maintenance Tip

Feeding Ornamental Saltwater Fish

Feed large saltwater fish two to three times per day. In the wild, most marine fish have a widely varied diet, and in a teeming ocean environment, food is plentiful. Watch closely, on a regular basis, to be sure all the fish are getting their share. Any fish that suddenly stops eating should be monitored for signs of disease or other stress. Generous feeding of a proper diet helps ensure long-term health, but can lead to water quality problems, hence the need for a sufficient and well-designed filtration system.

System Requirements for the Decorative Saltwater Aquarium

It simply cannot be emphasized enough that the key to success with saltwater aquariums is the proper design of the system. While it is possible to get by without some of the key equipment proposed in this book, always remember that marine aquarium fish are wild animals that have come from the ocean, and they are, therefore, wholly dependent on us for any chance at long-term survival in the home aquarium.

The system requirements for a healthy saltwater aquarium are well known. Nevertheless, many people still attempt to cut corners in ways that almost invariably end up costing more down the road than if they had simply invested in doing things right from the beginning. Consider that the average cost of a properly collected, shipped, and acclimatized saltwater fish is more than $150, and the math becomes quite clear. The loss of even a few fish due to a compromised system quickly exceeds the cost of purchasing the item in question in the first place.

The simplicity and flexibility of freshwater systems unfortunately does not apply to saltwater system design. There is just no way around it: Creating within the aquarium an environment as multifaceted and dynamic as the ocean demands certain devices and a level of investment and commitment from the very beginning.

A Case for Purity: Deionization and Reverse Osmosis

Osmosis Systems

For many reasons—old pipes, varying levels of treatment chemicals, pH variations, existence of toxins, heavy metals, sediment, and more—it is simply too risky to use tap water in an aquarium intended for delicate marine life. Because of the risks, it is standard practice to use pure, neutral-pH water as the foundation of the saltwater aquarium.

Acquiring pure water is, fortunately, a fairly easy process that can be achieved using one of two common methods: deionization or reverse osmosis (RO). Both methods achieve essentially the same result, but deionization systems leave virtually no wastewater, whereas RO units yield from 40 to 60 percent wastewater. Deionization systems also produce pure water on demand, right from the source, whereas RO units require more time for the purification process. RO units are much more compact, though, and that can be an advantage when space is a concern.

↓

It would not make sense to invest in such a sophisticated installation without investing equally in the proper equipment and system components. Research in advance to be sure the system requirements for long-term sustainability are within your budget.

In the end, both methods get the job done, and with a little independent research you can determine which one is right for you. The important thing to remember is that, in most instances, tap water is not suitable for use in saltwater aquariums, and if you plan to prepare your own saltwater for carrying out routine maintenance (water changes, for instance), a proper water treatment and purification system is a must. If a reputable professional aquarium maintenance service handles water changes, they are already using such a system. (Note that most residential water softener or filtration systems are unable to produce the pure, neutral water required by saltwater aquariums).

The Importance of
Using High-Quality Aquarium Salt

Although not part of the mechanical system, the salt added to the purified water is one of the essential components of a healthy, stable saltwater aquarium. Many brands of aquarium salt are available, and, as is true of most things, they are not necessarily created equal. There are cheap varieties, more expensive ones, and all the stops in between. Price does generally correlate with quality, but there are those who claim excellent results using less expensive brands. Does it really matter? There is certainly something to be said for salts that dissolve faster, are higher in essential trace minerals, and generally replace the necessary components that were removed in the water purification process. What is probably more important is to be consistent with the brand of salt you use; consistency tends to stability, which is the key to the successful saltwater aquarium.

Filtration

The modern decorative saltwater aquarium uses a combination of canister filters and a trickle or wet/dry filter (see chapter 3 for a full description of filter types), but the heart of the filtration system is the trickle filter. With its massive surface area for the colonization of beneficial bacteria, it is an ideal safeguard against major fluctuations in water quality that might result from the heavy feeding of and subsequent waste produced by large ornamental marine fish. The overflow box method (see page 36), which is necessary to move water from the aquarium to the trickle filter, is also used to move water below the aquarium and through other vital system components.

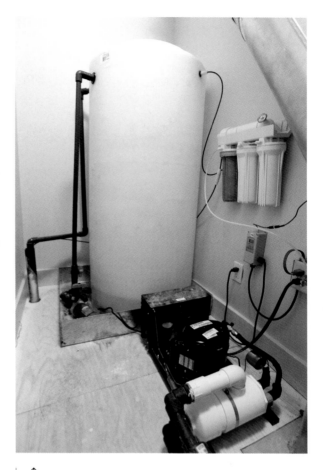

↑
This dedicated closet area stores the reverse osmosis system and mixing station so plenty of prepared saltwater is always available for water changes. While many aquarium maintenance companies and retailers provide or sell saltwater, there is no substitute for a ready supply on hand—especially for emergencies. In most cases, the system quickly pays for itself.

Lighting

Much of what is true for decorative freshwater aquarium lighting applies to the decorative saltwater style. Lighting options are many and varied and may involve any one or a combination of lighting types (see chapter 4 for more on lighting types). Because we are using light only to illuminate the aquarium, not to grow anything, a great deal of flexibility is possible. Bulbs offering spectrums high in the deeper blues are popular because they render the familiar characteristic blue color associated with seawater, but any lighting setup is feasible. One important consideration, however, is total wattage, or intensity of the light source, and how many hours per day the lights are continuously on. Too much light for too many hours per day always leads to excessive algae growth on the tank glass and decorative coral.

Do I Really Need That?
Specialized Equipment for Long-term Success

As interest in saltwater aquariums grows, so, too, does investment in new products and technologies to make them more accessible and successful. Though conflicting philosophies about the absolute need for some of the newer products do exist, the following items, for the most part, are fairly standard and consistently used by maintenance professionals.

Protein Skimmers
One piece of equipment that is standard issue for the modern saltwater aquarium is the protein skimmer. While some aquarists still try to get away with not installing this vital system component, too many well-documented benefits now exist to justify its exclusion from any serious saltwater installation.

Protein skimmers work by a process called foam fractionation. The venturi-style protein skimmer is the most common type. It works by using a dedicated pump to mix together air and water, in the process creating a foaming action that strips unwanted organics (toxins) from the aquarium water. A collection cup traps the separated organic waste and requires periodic emptying and rinsing (every few days or weekly, depending on the waste load), an easy process for most models. The soupy, green, and usually pungent water that fills the collection cup is evidence of the protein skimmer's effectiveness in removing organic waste. While it is possible to maintain a saltwater aquarium without a protein skimmer, using it ensures superior water conditions; in fact, it borders on foolish not to invest in one from the start.

↓

Here, both a trickle filter and a large canister filter are utilized.

Ultraviolet (UV) Sterilizers

Whereas the UV sterilizer is used for clarifying water in a fresh-water live-planted aquarium, its use in the decorative saltwater aquarium is foremost for killing pathogens and preventing many of the common diseases that plague ornamental saltwater fish. While some aquarists consider the UV sterilizers optional, it is another example of a device whose use offers another layer of protection. Although the UV sterilizers cannot prevent all diseases—and saltwater fish may become infected by other means or system shortcomings, even when a UV sterilizers is used—it certainly prevents and helps rid the aquarium of bacteria and disease-causing pathogens that find their way in.

For continued effectiveness, remember to replace the UV sterilizer bulb annually.

↖

Because of the nature and placement of this decorative saltwater aquarium, the filtration and system components were installed in a ventilated closet area a few feet away. The system should never be compromised for the sake of the installation.

→

Two popular models of protein skimmers

↓ ↘

Because this two-sided room divider installation is positioned near large windows, it receives a good deal of illumination through ambient light. For this reason, very low-wattage lighting is used over the aquarium to minimize algae growth.

Ozonizers

The ozonizer is probably the device least often used of those discussed here, but a general awareness of its existence is a good idea, especially if a large system with a heavy bioload (lots of big fish!) is desired. An ozonizer uses ozone to oxidize aquarium waste, which can rise as a result of overfeeding.

The ozonizer is controlled by a device called a redox meter/controller that measures the dissolved oxygen content in the water. As waste levels rise, oxygen content drops. The redox meter senses the drop in oxygen and triggers the ozonizer to release ozone into the water to maintain the correct oxygen level. Another trigger for ozone release might be a large fish dying behind a piece of coral or otherwise out of view. This can happen when you are of town and do not find the dead fish until it is already negatively affecting water quality. The ozone released helps oxidize the decaying fish and keep oxygen levels stable until it can be removed.

An ozone system is not a must-have for a successful tank, but it is a potentially worthwhile device that could buy valuable time in the event of a waste level overload.

Pursuing Ocean Purity: Maintenance Guidelines for the Decorative Saltwater Aquarium

It is the obligation of the homeowner, aquarium operator, or contracted maintenance professional to provide the highest standard of care possible for the sea creatures that are removed from their natural habitat for our enjoyment and appreciation.

When it comes to routine maintenance of the decorative saltwater aquarium, words like frequent and consistent cannot be emphasized enough. They are the hallmarks of clean, healthy, successful saltwater aquariums in which the wild and delicate inhabitants have the greatest chance of extended survival.

Water Changes

At a minimum, 30 percent of the aquarium water should be changed every two weeks. A best-case scenario is one where a small amount (20 to 25 percent) of water is changed once per week, but a regimen of 30 to 50 percent every two weeks—the general guideline standard for most professional aquarium maintenance companies—is also acceptable. As a general rule, though, you can't change water too often in a saltwater aquarium. Here, the need for and advantages of an on-site aquarium water-purification and salt-mixing station become glaringly obvious.

Monitoring Water Parameters

Due primarily to the high cost and vulnerability of ornamental saltwater fish, consistent monitoring of water parameters such as pH, salinity, alkalinity, and temperature are highly important. Excellent test kits and devices are readily available for these purposes.

Cleaning Decorative Coral

Depending on the intensity and duration of the daily lights-on period, decorative coral, over time, acquires algae. The point at which the coral requires cleaning—if at all—depends on your preference for the day-to-day appearance of the coral. Some people like the decorative coral to be pristinely clean at all times, while others choose to let it develop a nice algae patina, engaging only in the occasional cleaning. Some choose to never clean it, opting for a more natural look.

The best way to clean decorative coral is to soak it in a mild bleach solution, rinse it thoroughly, and then, if possible, soak the pieces in a mix of water and dechlorinator as an added safeguard against introducing residual bleach or chlorine into the aquarium. Another option is to maintain a second set of coral to use while the first is out for cleaning. If the algae growth on the removed coral is not too extreme, placing it in the sun for a few days is a natural way to eliminate the problem, although this technique can cause colored pieces to fade.

Other Routine Basics

Because so much equipment is needed for the decorative saltwater aquarium, it should be checked regularly for proper operation. Even if a professional service is hired to handle maintenance, saltwater aquarium fish and equipment require at least some level of the daily eye to monitor health and function. Examine fish closely for early signs of disease, such as white patchy growths, small sores, or, most commonly, ich. A parasite, ich looks like little grains of salt or white sand covering the fish's body. It starts out with a few spots that can be hard to see if you are not looking for it. Stopping ich in the early stages is vitally important because, in the marine aquarium, it can be very difficult to get rid of. Keep an eye on any scratches large fish acquire from scraping against rough decorative coral pieces; these can be entry points for infection.

Cleaning protein skimmer collection cups, rinsing or replacing particulate matter from overflow box sponges, and keeping an eye open for excessive buildup in the sump area of trickle filters are all part of good maintenance practice.

↑
A heavily stocked and pristinely clean aquarium, such as this one, quickly deteriorates without consistent and diligent maintenance. Be sure you have the time or money to invest in the proper care required to keep a saltwater aquarium healthy and stable.

→
A subtle hint of abstraction makes this aquarium not unlike a little sculpture, but its effectiveness depends on a bright, clean appearance.

Chapter 8:
Live Coral Reef Aquariums

The live coral reef aquarium represents the pinnacle of aquarium keeping. The beauty, diversity of life, and wonderful strangeness of the ocean reef environment captured within the aquarium is a wondrous sight. As a result of intense interest in natural coral reefs, reef aquariums are enjoying a huge spike in popularity, and immeasurable gains in knowledge, equipment, and specimen availability make them accessible worldwide. Who hasn't dreamed of having such an aquarium in the home after snorkeling or scuba diving an ocean reef or visiting a public aquarium? The allure is undeniable.

Unfortunately, because of the highly technical nature of live coral reef aquariums and the substantial knowledge base necessary to achieve success, they have remained largely the purview of seasoned hobbyists and aquarium professionals. But as more information, experience, and knowledge become available through books, the Internet, and a burgeoning reef aquarium club scene, this is changing. Basic formulas and requirements are better understood than they once were, and success is now possible for almost anyone willing to invest the time in keeping live coral reef aquariums.

←

The composition of this freestanding room divider installation is an underwater fusion of nature and design. The textured, stainless steel laminate cabinetry underscores the brilliance and hi-tech ambience of this live coral reef aquarium.

If your goal is to simply enjoy the visual feast—the grandeur and wonderful detail of a live coral reef aquarium—and leave the system design, installation, and long-term care to a professional aquarium service, you are in luck. As they do for decorative saltwater aquariums, companies exist that install and maintain reef aquariums exclusively, and they often have highly refined techniques acquired through experience. However, because you are the one who lives with the aquarium every day, it is important that you have a good grasp of what is involved in owning one. There is a start-up process to endure, and some necessary steps are required to achieve a reef aquarium that is a suitable, stable environment for its many amazing inhabitants.

You also want your aquarium to be an effective design element with a pleasing composition—more than a scattered arrangement of corals, rocks, and fish (which a reef aquarium can easily become). This chapter presents an overview of reef aquarium aesthetics and composition, popular corals and fish, and system and maintenance guidelines.

Aesthetic Considerations: The Impact of the Coral Reef Aquarium

A live coral reef aquarium can probably be integrated into just about any interior design style as long as it is viewed as a unique entity—as a stand alone fixture or sovereign focal point. Otherwise, its aesthetics may not pair well with many color tones and interior styles. In other words, this style of aquarium should be chosen for its unique inherent characteristics and not necessarily to harmonize with other interior elements.

The reason is simple. Live coral reef aquariums, by their sheer visual nature, have a defined presence. Unlike decorative freshwater and, to a lesser extent, decorative saltwater aquariums, options for lighting spectrums and effects or shades of interior components, such gravel and stones, do not exist. Instead, the reef aquarium teems with beautifully strange corals and the most colorful and varied of all aquarium fish. Its impact is at the heart of its design appeal.

The abstract forms of the corals and fish definitely lend reef aquariums the feel of modern art. A healthy and well-composed reef aquarium is not unlike a living, evolving work of sculpture, and it is easy to envision one in a modern, contemporary, or cosmopolitan interior.

A reef aquarium, with its great potential for visual complexity and rich detail, may also form an effective contrast to a minimalist interior style. This is not to say that a reef aquarium is limited to a particular aesthetic—its uniqueness and its ocean theme transcend design categorization—but total harmony

↑
The impact of a live coral reef aquarium on the space can be overwhelming. When incorporating a live reef aquarium into your space, you must decide early on whether your priority is harmony with the surroundings or simply an amazing aquarium regardless of prevailing aesthetics.

↑
Creating a U-shaped rock structure establishes a clear sense of how the aquascape should come together in terms of coral placement and overall emphasis.

of the reef aquarium with the surrounding space, should that be the goal, might be more difficult to achieve within certain interior design philosophies.

It is important to know that reef aquariums are bright. This is due to the high-wattage lighting required to grow and sustain the live corals. The light requirements are fixed, both in terms of duration and intensity (similar to the freshwater live-planted aquarium discussed in chapter 6). Because the aquarium needs to stay on a fixed cycle, viewing opportunities outside the set times are few. Even if the aquarium is illuminated with low-wattage lighting during hours intended solely for off-peak viewing, the corals begin to close up, resulting in a fairly lackluster scene.

Reef Building: Composition and Layout Approaches

There are a number of ways to compose a live coral reef aquarium, most of which either involve or are dictated by the nature of the installation itself. The aquascape must serve its viewing purpose, whether the aquarium is a room divider, island, freestanding, or built-in with a frontal view only.

Live Rock Architecture: The Foundation of the Coral Reef Aquarium Layout

The primary compositional shape of a reef aquarium is largely determined by the layout of the underlying rock structure. The most desirable material to use for this base structure is live rock. While this rock usually comes from ocean reefs, collection is strictly regulated (for obvious reasons) and often limited to rubble zones just outside of the primary reef area.

Although quality varies regionally, most live rock adds to the diversity and natural beauty of the aquascape by bringing with it many tiny life-forms and attractive higher-form algae. In many ways, the base material that forms the foundation of a natural reef is the same as that used in the reef aquarium.

The layout of the live rock base structure is, perhaps, the most important initial step in the construction of the aquascape of the live coral reef aquarium. Many elements, such as the corals, can be moved and rearranged until ideal placement is achieved. But the live rock base structure is a fixed foundation, and, although it can, theoretically, be adjusted or changed later, this significant undertaking is best done with few or no inhabitants in the aquarium at the time. In other words, the idea is to get it right the first time! It pays to know what compositional direction you want take from the earliest stages of planning and placing the live rock.

↑
A model slope-style layout. It can be tricky to fill the space at the high point because light penetration here is somewhat compromised. Choose corals with a good tolerance for low light conditions, or simply emphasize other areas of the composition.

Slope Style: Depth and Support from Sloped Foundations

The live rock base structure in an aquarium that is taller than 18 inches (46 cm) usually must slope downward. This provides solid support for the upper sections and keeps the structure as a whole from collapsing. A well-executed slope also enhances a feeling of depth and perspective in the layout. Of course, the nature of the slope depends on the type of installation.

Primary viewing angles also influence the composition of the base structure. A room divider demands a much different execution than a peninsula-style installation, for example. (See chapter 2 for aquarium styles.)

This dizzying array of corals is placed with precision and an understanding of their best location in the aquascape.

Design Tip

Getting Creative with Slopes

Try arranging the base rock to give the impression of a rolling underwater terrain, with peaks and valleys of varying heights and depths. Alternatively, create a steep sloping cliff that descends one side of the aquarium and leaves some open space on the opposite end.

Coral Placement

The corals are the major feature of the reef aquarium style, and their proper placement within the layout is important not only for creating a pleasing composition but also for their health. The optimal placement of any specimen requires a sense of what looks best as well as a firm knowledge of where in the aquascape that coral will do best.

There are three key points to consider when placing coral. One is distance from the light source: Some corals need intense light, while others do better nearer the bottom of the aquarium. Another is strength of the current (water flow): Some species open fully in areas of direct current only, while others prefer calmer areas of the aquarium. Last is the coral's compatibility with other corals: Some species harm others if their polyps touch or they otherwise come in contact. Because many new coral species are just now finding their way into the hobby, many of these interactions are still not entirely understood. How the newer corals react in close proximity to better-known corals has yet to be observed or formally documented. For now, we rely heavily on the dissemination of information gathered through the observations and experiences of aquarists.

It quickly becomes apparent that knowing what one is doing when dealing with live coral reef aquariums involves highly specific information about topics seemingly beyond the scope of any one book or instructional video. (Your exposure or otherwise to issues such as these goes a long way toward your decision to take on a reef aquarium yourself or seek the services or consultation of an aquarium professional.)

→
This mature coral reef aquarium shows how rich in detail, texture, and color these displays can be. Imagine looking at a scene like this from your sofa or dining room table.

←
This dizzying array of corals is placed with precision and an understanding of their best location in the aquascape.

Living Treasures: Common Live Corals and Other Invertebrates

The world's ocean reefs are home to countless species of live coral and other invertebrates, and a great many of them do quite well in a properly equipped and maintained reef aquarium. In many respects, these animals, with their rich textures and unusual forms, become design statements within the aquarium.

The following sections cover some of the well-known and commonly available species of soft and stony corals, shrimps, clams, and other interesting creatures for the reef aquarium. A general sense of their appearance and core requirements is a good starting point for envisioning your own live coral reef dreamscape. Keep in mind that, even among experts, the precise naming and categorization of many aquarium corals is not firmly established, so this discussion on corals is limited to general groups and common names. With these names, you should be able find what you're looking for from a supplier or designer.

Soft Corals

Soft corals are those without a hard skeleton or skeletal base from which polyps extend. These corals are essentially tissue and water, and they regulate the amount of water within their bodies by expanding and contracting over the course of a day. When the aquarium lights first come on, soft corals usually look shrunken and a bit droopy, but after a few hours in good conditions they expand into full form—effectively tripling in size—only to shrink toward the end of the day or photoperiod.

Take this dramatic size change into account when placing soft corals in the aquascape. In the wild, these corals are generally found at greater depths on the reef, so they require less intense light; the best placement is toward the lower middle and bottom regions of the aquarium.

Mushrooms

Mushroom polyps are among the hardiest invertebrates, and the easiest to care for, in the reef aquarium. They come in so many types that naming cannot be standardized, so the generic term mushroom can refer to specimens of great color and texture variance. Some, such as the elephant ear mushroom, can grow very large, reaching a diameter of 24 inches (60 cm) or more, while others, at only 1 to 2 inches (2.5 to 5 cm), stay quite small. These smaller types are sold attached to rocks, whose surfaces can often support multiple specimens of either the same species or three or four varieties.

Leather Corals

Named for their leathery texture and neutral, muted colors, leathers are an exceptionally hardy group of soft corals. They prefer areas of reasonably high current and good lighting—two elements typically in abundance in a well-designed reef system—so placement options abound. It should be noted, though, that many of these corals can inhibit the growth of, or even kill, other coral types around them—but only if placed too close. Otherwise, they are dependable reef aquarium inhabitants that can be used rather freely, especially to fill in gaps in the layout.

Colt Corals

These corals are hardy and can grow large in the aquarium. Their soft, fleshy appearance projects a beautiful swaying elegance in the strong currents they prefer. It is important to give them sufficient area to expand throughout the day or photoperiod, because what starts out looking like a relatively small specimen can quickly expand to more than double that size. Colt corals also make an attractive and effective centerpiece or focal point in the composition.

↗

Because they prefer less intense light and a slower current, colorful mushroom polyps are an excellent choice for the lower portions of the composition, especially the bottom, where fewer other species can thrive (top).

↗

A giant elephant ear mushroom. At night, this monster curls into a ball about the size of a grapefruit. By midday, it stretches to more than 18 inches (46 cm).

↗

A specimen umbrella coral, a type of leather coral. Although not the most colorful of corals, its size and texture adds a lot to the overall coral composition.

→

A clownfish frolics in a giant colt coral.

↑
The light tips of this branchy *Acropora* sp. coral show where it has grown since being in the aquarium. Taking a break, a flame hawkfish has nestled into the coral's base.

Stony Corals

When most people think of coral, they think of its hard skeletal casing rather than the extending polyps. But the polyps are the living tissue of the coral or coral colony. Stony corals are those that produce the hard exoskeleton of calcium carbonate with which we are familiar. Unlike soft corals, when a stony coral dies, the exoskeleton remains.

Generally speaking, stony corals can be divided into two groups (although some species fall in between): small-polyp stony corals and large-polyp stony corals, often referred to as SPS and LPS respectively.

Small-polyp stony corals (SPS) have the largest amount of exoskeleton, some species requiring close examination to see the actual polyps. Their fixed, rigid appearance offers a contrast to the flowing movement of the soft corals. SPS corals should be placed at the topmost portions of the aquarium, as they demand the intense light and steady, strong currents found there. Conditions must be close to ideal for most coral species to thrive; this is especially true for the SPS corals.

The distinguishing feature of large-polyp stony corals (LPS) is, of course, their large polyps. Far less of the exoskeleton is visible, so their applications within the coral reef aquarium center on the

artful display of the polyps. LPS corals include varying and quite dramatic polyp forms, giving them an edge in terms of variety, color, shape, and especially placement options. An attractive species is available for just about every stratum of the aquarium. This is the group of corals you are likely to find most heavily represented in reef aquariums.

Listing every available coral species is outside the scope of this book, so what follows is a look at some of the common species that gives a feel for what is available. In many respects, learning about a few specific species can help you deduce a good deal about similar species. A wealth of detailed information about practically every coral kept in home reef aquariums can be found. (See the Resources guide beginning on page 170.)

Design Tip

Using Neutral Colors in the Reef Aquarium
The browns and cream tones of many hardy soft corals are an effective counterpoint to the vivid iridescence of other coral species. Neutral colors help balance the composition and can prevent an overly gaudy appearance.

Acropora

As a group, *Acropora* is among the most common of the SPS corals. Placed at the top of the layout, their jutting and angular antlerlike appearance gives a reef aquarium the natural, stratified look of a real ocean reef. *Acropora* species are always found in shallow-water reefs or near the surface, so similar placement in the aquarium is a must.

Cup Coral

The cup coral is a remarkable SPS coral. These corals have a rigid structure, and the polyps are not especially visible, so theirs is often a textural role. They can easily be placed in narrow or tricky areas of the live rock structure, filling gaps with slivers of color.

Brain Corals

Brain corals fall into two main types: closed and open. Obviously named for their resemblance to the human brain, their distinctive patterns are a fine textural variants for any live coral reef aquarium. The closed varieties are generally easier to care for and among the hardiest of corals.

Open brain coral makes an impressive addition and can be an exceptional focal specimen in a reef aquarium composition. Their preference for low-current areas makes them a good choice for the middle and lower regions of the aquascape.

Bubble Coral

A lovely and distinctive LPS coral, the bubble coral is easily recognizable by its large inflated tissues, which look like bubbles gathered on a stony base. Some specimens assume an attractive greenish iridescence that is quite striking. Bubble corals do well nestled in low current areas, but for optimal enjoyment of their distinctive form, give them plenty of exposure.

Hammer and Frogspawn Corals

The hammer coral, with its brilliant green and tan polyps, provides a distinctive LPS presence to the live coral reef aquascape. The polyps have a graphic, textilelike shape with an almost futuristic design quality—especially noticeable when multiple specimens are placed together to form a larger group. However, be sure to give them adequate space, so they do not readily touch other coral species.

Frogspawn coral, another LPS, is a close relative to hammer coral and projects a similar appeal. Its gelatinous polyps are appropriately named, for they bear a resemblance to a cluster of frog eggs.

A splash of aquamarine from this cup coral.

←

An example of a closed brain coral

→

An example of an open brain coral

↓
This bubble coral's nice green tint is contributed by the beneficial algae that live within its tissues (middle).

↓
Hammer and frogspawn corals prefer moderate current and light conditions, so placement options are plentiful (right).

Gorgonian Corals

Gorgonians are a coral form completely different from stony or soft corals; they are identifiable by their unmistakable branches. Visually, they serve as a wonderful final touch to the coral composition because they can often be positioned in areas where other coral types cannot. Their tall, branchy posture is useful also for adding depth and dimension to the aquascape.

Noncoral Invertebrates for the Reef Aquarium

Although live corals play the lead role in the reef aquarium, many other equally interesting invertebrates bring great diversity as well, contributing to an aquascape that closely replicates the wonders of a teeming coral reef. Here is a look at some of them.

Tridacna Clams

These giant clams (in the wild, some grow to be 2 feet [61cm] long and live for more than 100 years, although you shouldn't expect this in the aquarium) show myriad intricate patterns and stunning pigmentation in their blue and green iridescence. Although they require a lot of light, they must often be placed on the aquarium bottom so they can open and close freely without the threat of falling from the rock structure.

Feather Dusters

Feather Dusters are actually a type of tubeworm. They extend their feathery plumes into the current to feed on organic particulate matter. Not always noticeable from a distance, they are among the many detailed invertebrates that make close-up observation of a reef aquarium so satisfying.

Anemones

Anemones are generally discouraged for reef aquariums, which may surprise newcomers to this style. The primary reason is that anemones have the potential to move about the aquarium. If they don't like where they are placed, they are liable to move to a more suitable location—suitable to the anemone, that is! This not only plays havoc on the composition, it puts prized corals—which the anemones can sting—in harm's way.

Cleaners

As with the freshwater live-planted aquarium and its resident cleaning crew of algae-eating shrimps, O-cats, and others (see chapter 6), the reef aquarium has its own function-specific creatures that control algae and perform sifting and polishing duties. Many of these animals are quite attractive and are interesting to watch up close.

Cleaners include Astrea snails, various shrimps, red-legged and blue-legged hermit crabs, and sand-sifting starfish. To a large extent, these cleaners should be viewed as essential components of a modern reef aquarium for their practical applications. It is merely a bonus that they are also so interesting and beautiful. Noncleaning shrimps, starfishes, and crabs may also be added for purely ornamental purposes.

←

An exquisite purple-branching gorgonian coral

↑

Tridacna clams are otherworldly sea creatures for the home reef aquarium.

↗

Feather Dusters extend their graceful plumes to gather organic matter.

↓

Red-legged hermit crabs on duty

Maintenance Tip

Feeding Corals

Even if a professional service maintains the aquarium, feeding responsibilities usually fall to the aquarium owner. One important recent advancement in live coral maintenance is the availability of phytoplankton supplements, which are highly necessary nutrition for these invertebrates.

The Fish

As is true with the freshwater live-planted aquarium, the fish in the live coral reef aquarium typically play a complementary role in the composition. The best fish for the reef aquarium are generally much smaller and more peaceful than the large, more aggressive ornamental fish commonly used in the decorative saltwater aquarium. Most of these larger fish can wreak havoc on the delicate and precise positioning of corals and either eat corals as part of their natural diet or simply grow too large to move with grace in the typical reef aquarium arrangement.

Hundreds of small and medium-sized fish are available, however, and they are both exceedingly beautiful and balancing in the coral reef aquarium. We look at a few in the following section. Keep in mind that many groups of fish (the wrasses and tangs discussed in chapter 7, for example) have members suitable for both the decorative saltwater style and the reef aquarium.

Damsels and Chromis Species

Many damsel species stay small and are quite peaceful, while some, such as those discussed in chapter 7, can become fairly large and extremely territorial. Often, the behaviors of individual members of the same group of fish are so different that it is hard to believe they are related.

Green Chromis

With its lovely aquamarine green color and mild-mannered temperament, the green chromis (below) is a real staple of the reef aquarium. Green chromis do well in small groups and usually school or huddle together, an unusual trait among reef aquarium fish.

↓

These small reef fishes are comfortably at home in this large reef aquarium.

Neon Damsels

A striking little black fish, the neon damsel (below, left), is a fine addition to a large reef aquarium in its juvenile form (shown below, left). As it matures, the neon damsel will lose some of its blue coloration and may become more aggressive. However, that aggression is usually effectively countered when it is among larger wrasses and tangs.

Clownfish

Though technically categorized as damselfish, within the aquarium trade clownfish, or anemonefish, (below, right), are viewed and referred to as a separate group. An enduring favorite of reef aquarists and aquarium-lovers the world over, most clownfish enjoy frolicking in anemones and the extensions of many kinds of soft coral. They are a graphic symbol of small oceanic reef fish of all types.

False Percula Clownfish

Although true percula clownfish are available, they are rare and hard to come by (shown, below, right). The false percula, on the other hand, better represents what most people imagine when they think of the clownfish. Many clownfish available in today's aquarium trade are captive-bred rather than collected from the ocean. In lieu of having a host anemone present in the aquarium within which to play, they often frolic in the polyps of some corals. This can sometimes cause the coral to retract but is ultimately harmless.

Wrasses

Wrasses are a fish group with both reef-friendly and non-reef-friendly members. (Non-reef-friendly refers to species that are fine for a decorative saltwater aquarium but not recommended for a reef aquarium.) Fortunately, there are plenty of reef-friendly wrasses to choose from, and they are always popular due to their intricate body and swimming patterns.

Fairy Wrasse

Many reef-compatible wrasses are types of fairy wrasse. All are exceptionally colorful and readily available. Their bodies look like little swimming canvases with airbrushed or paintstroked patterns of random design.

Christmas Wrasse

The Christmas wrasse is a beautiful little reef fish with a pleasing pink and green striped body. Its expression suggests a curiosity corroborated by their appearing to always be exploring and investigating the many cracks and crevices of a reef aquarium.

Tangs

Another group discussed in detail in chapter 7, tangs are among the few groups of aquarium fish with members that can be kept in both decorative saltwater and reef aquariums, the yellow tang and powder-blue tang chief among them. In the reef aquarium, a few key species actually perform desirable algae-grazing and control functions. In fact, the naturally occurring algae in reef aquariums helps maintain healthy tangs, whose diets are often lacking in the decorative saltwater aquarium.

Pacific or Regal Blue Tang

Another classic fish of the reef, the regal blue tang has one of the deepest and purest blue colorations of any reef fish. Readily available juveniles do well in small groups, which can make an attractive display, but larger specimens often quarrel with one another.

Purple Tang

A deep bluish-purple body and bright yellow tail characterize this exceptional reef aquarium tang. They may scuffle a bit with other tangs in the aquarium, but are not especially aggressive, which some tangs used in reef aquariums (the Sohal tang, for example) can be.

Best Supporting Actors: Other Noteworthy Individuals for the Reef Aquarium

Each fish brings its own unique presence and allure to the live coral reef aquarium. In addition to the large groups of fish are a few individuals that are easily obtainable and very much at home in just about any reef aquarium and with just about any tankmates.

The flame hawkfish is an entertaining character. Because hawkfish have no swim bladder (the swim bladder keeps the fish buoyant), they must perch on rocks or other areas between their endearing flights from one spot to the next. The Mandarin goby, with its Chinese dragon markings and pursed mouth, is a fascinating character as well. And, of course, the royal gramma, which is actually a small member of the grouper family, is an all-time favorite.

Sources and availability of any given species vary by country and region, so it is always a good idea to do research on and learn about the fish available from your local suppliers. There are so many fishes for the reef aquarium that your choice is a simple matter of deciding what you like best.

↑
No reef aquarium is complete without a royal gramma.

↓
One of the most flamboyant little reef fishes, the mandarin goby appears dressed in a lavish costume.

A Most Delicate Balance: System Requirements for the Coral Reef Aquarium

Although many aspects of reef aquarium system design are similar to those used for decorative saltwater aquariums, there are a few differences. What remains the same is the importance of investing in proper high-quality equipment.

Filtration

For the most part, filtration and water treatment requirements for a reef aquarium are identical to those of the decorative saltwater aquarium style discussed in chapter 7. The only real difference is that in the sump (or, in the decorative saltwater style, the trickle filter) of a reef aquarium system, no form of biological filter medium is used. This is because the primary biological filtration (see chapter 3) takes place in the aquarium through the live rock.

Live rock is chock-full of good bacteria that handle the biological filtration process at a more natural and advantageous pace than a (potentially) over efficient biological filter medium placed in a trickle filter. The trickle filter can process waste too quickly, causing the potential for an undesirable buildup of nitrate, the end product of the nitrogen cycle (see page 35). Excess nitrate in the reef aquarium is tempered by the somewhat less efficient but, again, more natural breakdown of waste by microorganisms contained in the live rock.

Using a UV sterilizer is also neither necessary nor advised for a live coral reef aquarium. It is believed to eliminate too many of the good microorganisms necessary for the proper function of these dynamic contained environments.

Lighting

Another area in which the saltwater reef aquarium parallels the freshwater live-planted aquarium is in lighting. In both aquarium styles, the lighting is more than mere illumination; it is like the Sun, an indispensable life source for a great many reef aquarium inhabitants.

Many corals and other invertebrates harbor symbiotic algae known as zooxanxthellate within their tissues. These important algae require sufficient full-spectrum lighting to engage in photosynthesis, the process of converting light energy into nutrition used by live coral. This process is fundamental to the survival of live corals and other invertebrates that harbor zooxanxthellate algae (the attractive and popular Tridacna clam, for example).

Lighting duration (the photoperiod) is equally important in the reef aquarium. Unlike the illumination for freshwater or decorative saltwater aquarium styles, the light source must be consistent and constant each day. An average of ten hours per day is ideal. Many aquarists employ a more natural daylight cycle whereby lighting intensity is sequenced in a sort of dawn-to-dusk cycle. Low-wattage lights come on first (sunrise), are later joined by higher-wattage sources (midday/afternoon), and then go back to low-wattage or limited-source lighting (evening/sunset). While this method has not proven necessary, it stands to reason that any feasible replication of natural conditions within the aquarium would be beneficial.

Lighting Types

The modern live coral reef aquarium typically uses at least two light sources. Although it is certainly possible to meet the needs of some smaller systems with just one light fixture or source,

to effectively cover the range of light intensity and spectral requirements of a reef system, a combination of halide and high-output fluorescent lighting is best. The recommended average ratio is 4 to 8 watts of light per gallon (3.8 Liters) of water. HQI halogen lighting is especially beneficial for its remarkable intensity and depth penetration.

When in doubt about how much light is sufficient, it is better to err on the side of higher wattage and greater intensity from the light source.

Actinic 03

Although they are used for aesthetic or decorative lighting in other aquarium styles, actinic 03 lamps are essential in the reef aquarium. These bulbs are high in the blue spectrums, which best penetrate seawater and encourage the photosynthetic processes of the zooxanxthellate algae within the coral. It is possible to achieve a concentrated blue with a single lamp, such as a 20,000 K metal halide, but more often, the blue spectrum is supplemented with actinic 03 bulbs—usually in the form of very high output (VHO) fluorescents. These bulbs also project a subtle but effective bluish cast that diminishes the harshness of metal halide lighting.

↑

Strong actinic lighting gives this reef aquarium a blue cast. A common practice is to finish the photoperiod with a short period of actinic lighting alone.

↓

This aquarium features a typical combination of metal halide and VHO fluorescent lighting systems. The metal halide system handles the primary light requirements; the VHOs supply the actinic 03 additional blue spectrum.

↑

An acrylic box like this serves as the sump or reservoir to which the main recirculation pump is attached, like a trickle filter system. From this sump area, water is moved through vital system components such as the protein skimmer and chiller.

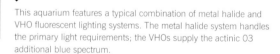

Fusing Nature and Technology:
Specialized Electronics for the Reef Aquarium

No other aquarium style has seen the advancements in dedicated computer monitoring devices, software, and other specialized electronic equipment that reef aquariums have. This is likely due to the more sophisticated systems and the high level of investment involved in installing, stocking, and maintaining a reef aquarium. A well-stocked 200- to 300-gallon (757- to 1,135-liter) reef aquarium may contain more than $5,000 (£2845) in livestock, an investment worth protecting.

Devices exist that monitor every essential function, provide real-time data, and maintain daily cycle histories. Many can be connected to remote laptop computers or mobile phones and sound alarms or send warning messages when programmed levels for any given parameter (temperature or pH, for instance) go too far up or down. These rapidly advancing technologies are reflected daily in new and improved devices and software.

Wave-makers

The constant movements of waves are a significant part of the natural coral reef dynamics. To more closely simulate natural wave and tidal actions, simple but clever devices have been developed for reef aquariums. Essentially a timer-based system, the wave-maker consists of a series of control modules connected to several specially positioned pumps inside the aquarium. The programmed on/off cycles of the pumps create natural back-and-forth currents, yielding three benefits. One is simply the pleasing, natural look of the corals swaying as they would in a real ocean environment. Another is that the sequenced shifting of the current in the aquarium prevents the formation of dead zones—areas that established or fixed currents do not reach. Finally, the shifting current provided by a wave-maker system keeps detritus (debris) from settling in any one spot in the aquarium.

Caring for the Indoor Ocean: Maintenance Guidelines for Live Coral Reef Aquariums

In a natural ocean reef, water is constantly moving; currents, tides, and waves, plus the ocean's vast size, keep the reef environment perpetually clean in a way that cannot be duplicated in a home aquarium. Because aquariums are closed systems, their dynamics and variables are different from those of the ocean. Thus, although we look to nature to tell us what conditions are desirable, we must devise our own methods and means of achieving them.

↑
Advances in technology affect many areas of our lives, including aquariums. New and better aquarium monitoring systems that help maintain more stable systems are emerging.

To this end, a number of approaches have been devised to deal with routine maintenance regimens for reef aquariums. A little research, however, reveals conflicting theories. Although all of the theories purport to be effective, often that effectiveness is directly linked to strict adherence to a particular program, system, or established school of thought (of which there are many when it comes to live coral reef aquariums). Here, we look at a few simple guidelines that take into account the common threads among several approaches to reef aquarium maintenance.

Water Changes

You cannot change too much water in a reef aquarium. With the will, the facility, and the budget, small water changes of 20 percent or so made daily or every other day benefit the reef aquarium (provided sufficient supplements are added regularly). But a more common and more manageable routine employs a 30 to 40 percent water change every ten to fourteen days. A survey of several professional aquarium maintenance companies reveals this as the average amount and frequency of water changes required to maintain consistency and keep the overall appearance of the aquarium "very good to excellent."

Other Routine Maintenance

In addition to regularly removing algae from aquarium walls and cleaning the protein skimmer collection cup, you should keep an eye open for fallen corals, especially when they are recently added. Because corals are simply placed in pockets and openings in the live rock structure, they do not always achieve perfect stability. Most corals can handle the occasional tumble, but if one keeps falling over, seek a different place for it.

Lightbulbs should be replaced every six months to one year. While they may still appear bright to our eyes, full-spectrum lamps slowly diminish in intensity and spectrum over time, and the corals may start to experience the effects of insufficient light well before our eyes perceive a change. It is generally better to change bulbs sooner rather than later, because letting them go too long (one to two years) allows them to become too dim; the sudden return to full intensity and brightness when they are finally changed can contribute to algae problems and shock the invertebrates.

Other routine tasks, such as adding supplements for corals and checking or cleaning probes attached to monitoring devices, may also be necessary. The level of maintenance you perform depends on the approach or philosophy you adopt for a particular aquarium and whether or not you hire a professional service for routine maintenance. If you do, the service technician may alert you to special tasks you should perform between visits. A little research reveals lots of tips and tricks that apply to specific system types.

↑
A collection of brain, leather, and bubble corals thrives under optimum conditions.

↓
Just after a water change, a reef aquarium takes on a striking clarity. This 350-gallon (1,324-liter) display is packed with corals and fish. There is little room for lax maintenance practices.

Part 04: Case Studies

In this section, we take a detailed look at several aquarium styles in a variety of settings and with differing installation applications. Background information provides insight into each aquarium's conception.

Chapter 9 focuses on freshwater aquariums and illuminates the ways in which this versatile style can work in a wide variety of décors. Chapter 10, which covers saltwater aquariums, shows the beauty of a contained marine environment—as a source of wonder and a complement to the space.

Metropolitan Home Decorative Freshwater Aquarium

The idea to incorporate an aquarium into this stylish metropolitan home came from the interior designer, who had used aquariums on previous projects with great results. Because the home was still in the blueprint phase when the aquarium was suggested, the architect was able to easily incorporate it into the floor plan. Moreover, now the designer, architect, and client had the benefit of developing their ideas about the space knowing that it would include an aquarium. This served to hone the aquarium's desired effect and allowed a clearer vision to be conveyed to the aquarium design and installation company. In the end, good design forethought went a long way toward creating an aquarium at one with the space.

The aquarium is positioned in an open-ended dividing wall and is visible from the entrance foyer. A comfortable reading area is on this side as well. The other primary view, from a combination seating/dining area, gives the aquarium considerable presence throughout the first floor.

This decorative freshwater aquarium is a hardscape-only design featuring a combination of fossilized rock and thin, branchy driftwood. In this two-section composition, the rock serves as the support structure for the driftwood. Angling the driftwood creates a suggestion of water flowing through the aquarium, as if natural currents were causing the wood to lean slightly. The fine, muted-color gravel was chosen for its similarity to the rock; it looks like a product of natural erosion.

Fish species were limited to avoid crowding the scene and distracting from the aquascape. German koi angelfish proved the perfect accompaniment, their markings and colorations punctuating the urban organic feel of the interior. Two small schools of tetras complete the composition.

Maintenance is minimized by the absence of artificial plants, which tend to show algae growth more readily than rocks and driftwood. The photoperiod is limited to the primary viewing hours each day, though a simple remote switch allows the lights to be easily turned on any time. Routine water changes are uncomplicated due to the integrated drain hole and fill faucet located under the aquarium.

←
A pleasing composition with accents in all the right places. This composition inspires quiet contemplation from the many surrounding seating areas.

Aquarium System and Installation Data

Aquarium Material:
Glass

Aquarium Dimensions:
60" × 30" × 37.5"
(152 cm × 76 cm × 95 cm)
Support stand height: 36" (90 cm)

Aquarium Volume:
290 gallons (1,098 liters)

Lighting:
Two 48" (120 cm), 110-watt,
10,000 K, VHO fluorescents
(220 watts total)

Filtration:
Trickle filter, powered by Iwaki model
30 (flow) magnet-drive pump; one
Eheim model 2260 large-capacity
canister-style filter, plumbed through
aquarium bottom

Substrate:
Fine quartz-based decorative gravel

Fish:
German koi angelfish (*Pterophyllum*
sp. hybrid); rummy-nose tetras
(*Hemigrammus bleheri*)

Water Change:
Every two weeks, 50 percent
of tank volume

↓
The aquarium is the focal point of this seating area. The hardscape
materials work well with the displayed accessories. Overall tones in
the aquarium harmonize with the room.

↑
A bright spot in a warm-toned room, the aquarium adds life, movement, and color.

↑
This room is just off the foyer, so the aquarium is visible upon entering the home. The space is a relaxing reading and music area to which the aquarium is an inspired complement.

↑
The stark marbled pattern and yellow crown distinguish the koi angelfish. The particular coloration of this angelfish hybrid is ideal for the prevailing tones of this space.

↑
The branched driftwood fills the aquarium interior height without blocking views between the rooms.

↑
A combination trickle filter and canister setup provides superb filtration. The hose running from the fill faucet to the drain hole protects against drips and water damage. The pink and yellow foam padding dampens noise.

↑
The access door props open, allowing plenty of room for aquascaping and routine maintenance.

Cherrywood Bedroom
Decorative Freshwater Aquarium

A masculine cherrywood bedroom is the setting for a decorative freshwater aquarium whose aquascape and installation echoes the bold theme and heavy wood feel. Although this aquarium was the homeowner's idea, he sought the expert assistance of a professional aquarium designer and installation firm to make manifest his vision. The goal was to give a freestanding aquarium a built-in look by emphasizing the cabinetry and making it look like the aquarium was part of the original design of the home. The result is an aquarium whose craftsmanship enhances and adds life to the room.

The hardscape, a combination of thick pieces of red driftwood and light-colored stone, not only matches the aquarium to the space but also provides sufficient retreat for the fish. In areas of intermittent activity, such as a bedroom, fish may be frightened when someone suddenly enters the room. A layout with plenty of hiding spaces keeps fish comfortable and healthy. The substrate is fine-grade white quartz gravel, which reflects the aquarium light and provides brightness—a welcome contrast to the dark cherry furniture.

The main group of fish comprises large African cichlids; they are accompanied by red hooks, whose muted color and shape contrast nicely with the colorful cichlids. Rainbow sharks, T-barbs, and loaches round out the selection.

Artificial plants provide color and texture in the aquarium. The plant style is limited to tall, vertical shapes that fill in the background without completely concealing it, a technique that adds depth to the aquascape.

In a room with little artwork on the walls and few accessories, this well-designed, low-maintenance, decorative freshwater aquarium functions as the primary design element.

←

A bright spot in a warm-toned room, the aquarium adds life, movement, and color.

Aquarium System and Installation Data

Aquarium Material:
Glass

Aquarium Dimensions:
84" × 24" × 24"
(214 cm × 60 cm × 60 cm)
Support stand height: 42" (107 cm)

Aquarium Volume:
200 gallons (757 liters)

Lighting:
Two 72" (183 cm), 155-watt 50/50
VHO fluorescents (310 watts total)

Filtration:
Two Eheim model 2260 large-capacity canister-style filters, plumbed through aquarium bottom

Substrate:
Fine-grained quartz gravel

Fish:
Electric blue Ahli, lemon-yellow Labidichromis, German red peacock, sunshine peacock, rainbow shark, Botia loachata, clown loach, red hook, T-barb

Water Change:
Every two weeks, 50 percent of tank volume

←
Although this is a freestanding aquarium, the designer produced an integrated appearance by taking the cabinetry a step beyond the stand-and-canopy installation. In fact, the custom-built aquarium cabinetry looks like part of the original bedroom set.

↑
A perfect view from the bed allows the homeowner to relax while watching the aquarium or to read and enjoy its ambient effects. Placement anywhere else in this room would not have produced these optional views.

↑
The top door opens and slides back into the cabinet for maximum access and to prevent bumping one's head while servicing the aquarium. When one feeds the fish, the door needs to be lifted only slightly.

↑
Sufficiently masculine in temperament to match the overall theme of the room, African cichlids form the primary group of fish. They also add an exciting burst of color to a fairly monotone space.

↑
Because the aquarium is 84 inches (213 cm) long and the light fixtures are 60 inches (152 cm), the 6 inches (15 cm) of space at each end of the aquarium creates a natural shadow area. Tapering the hardscape at each end emphasizes this compositional feature.

↑
Two large canister filters maintain excellent water vquality. Plumbing through the bottom eliminates filter encumbrances from the aquascape.

↑
This aquarium is the ultimate nightlight.

Eclectic-Style Home Decorative Freshwater Aquarium

The proud owner of this inspired decorative freshwater aquarium wanted a unique composition that utilized few species in great contrast. A long-time fish hobbyist and aficionado, he was familiar with exotic cichlid species from both lakes Malawi and Tanganyika, and sought to combine two prized classics—*Frontosas* from Lake Tanganyika and lemon-yellow *Labidochromis* from lake Malawi. The two species came together with surprising effectiveness in a large, freestanding bowfront aquarium with custom-made stand and matching canopy top. Positioned in a seating area just off the bar and living room, the aquarium is the topic of conversation whenever the homeowner entertains guests and family, which he does often. This aquarium is a design statement as unusual as the space it occupies.

Lace rock forms the background wall and several midground caves, which are welcome retreats for the fish. *Frontosas*, prized for their muscular appearance and blue-tinged fins, form the large group of dark brown and tan striped fish. A perfect group of beaming lemon-yellow *Labidochromis* form a wonderful contrast with the *Frontosas*. Dispersed throughout the composition are a few select peacock cichlids, which provide variety and visual interest without getting in the way of the primary fish theme. A pair of rare catfish provide just the right amount of whimsy to render the aquascape as eclectic as the rest of the home.

The substrate is a salt-and-pepper blend of fine sand specially made for cichlid aquariums. Its brightness pairs well with the dark lace rock. The lighting, a strong blue, is a bit atypical for freshwater aquariums, but it works beautifully here nonetheless. Wattage is kept low to maintain a slightly subdued environment.

Maintenance is easy due to the absence of artificial plants, which show algae growth and can be dislodged by large fish. Smoothing the sand, removing algae from the glass, and changing 50 to 75 percent of the water every two weeks keeps the aquarium in top form. The rock structure has never had to be moved for any reason; periodic adjustments are all that are necessary.

←

A one-of-a-kind aquarium in a one-of-a-kind space. The versatility of the decorative freshwater style is evident.

→

The bowed front glass adds useful depth and dimension.

Aquarium System and Installation Data

Aquarium Material:
Glass

Aquarium Dimensions:
96" × 36" × 36"
(244 cm × 91 cm × 91 cm)
Support stand height: 36" (90 cm)

Aquarium Volume:
540 gallons (2,043 liters)

Lighting:
Two 165-watt, 10,000 K VHO
fluorescents; two 165-watt actinic
03 VHO fluorescents

Filtration:
Trickle filter powered by magnet-drive
pump; two Eheim model 2260 large-
capacity canister filters, plumbed
through tank bottom

Substrate:
Fine white sand with black grains

Fish:
Frontosa, lemon-yellow
Labidichromis, electric blue ahli,
sunshine peacock, German red
peacock, catfish species

Water Change:
Every two weeks, 50 to 75
percent of tank volume

Special Equipment:
25-watt UV sterilizer

Contrast and harmony are evident with this fish selection. The white-and-black sand coupled with the fish colors give the composition a marine feel.

Large, flat pieces of lace rock along the back of the aquarium give depth without bulk, and leave the midground and foreground open. This allows plenty of swimming space for the large *Frontosas*, and permits hiding behind and between rocks, a natural need for cichlids.

Removing the canopy top for this large freestanding aquarium requires two people. The two VHO fixtures provide excellent light while maintaining a low profile. Because it does not have to clear a large light fixture, the canopy top can be made shorter (and lighter).

A UV sterilizer is included on this system for disease prevention and water clarity.

Dockside Home
Live-Planted Aquarium

The owners of this home were looking for an aquarium in the discus live-planted aquarium style, as they were drawn to the peaceful allure of planted aquariums but wanted larger ornamental fish with character. A discus live-planted aquarium was the perfect solution. Through collaboration with the aquarium service and their interior designer, they settled on the final design. The resulting installation, a focal point of the space, is impossible to miss on entering the room.

The freestanding aquarium with matching canopy top anchors the space and its relaxed and inviting interior. The open floor plan enables views from the entryway, formal dining area, living room, and kitchen. The front of the aquarium is bowed glass, which gives the tank an elegant air. Matched cabinetry and paint lend an integrated, planned appearance. Lots of windows with views to the docks outside establish a water theme—which the aquarium accents—but also create considerable glare, so the aquarium was positioned to minimize the effects during the daytime.

The layout of the aquarium is uncomplicated. It establishes an unfettered, orderly backdrop for the real stars of this aquarium: the discus. Because the space has a lot of design accessories, the streamlined aquascape provides uncluttered balance. The rock arrangement acts as a barrier between the foreground sand and the substrate in the back for the live plants. Using only two medium-sized pieces of driftwood helps keep the design spare. This benefits the discus, too, as a more complex arrangement would crowd the aquarium and compromise swimming space.

Because of the discus' demand for exceptional water quality, maintenance is frequent, but not difficult, due to the sole use of sword plants, which require nothing more than thinning the older outer leaves. No major trimming or extended periods working inside the aquarium are necessary. The appearance of the aquascape remains constant, a rare feature of the live-planted aquarium style. The homeowners have the benefit of knowing that, with proper long-term care, their aquarium will remain vibrant and beautiful for years to come.

←
This discus live-planted aquarium is the focal point of this formal dining room and an inspiring conversation piece.

Aquarium System and Installation Data

Aquarium Material:
Glass

Aquarium Dimensions:
72" × 28" × 30"
(180 cm × 70 cm × 76 cm)
Support stand height: 42" (107 cm)

Aqua Volume:
260 gallons (985 liters)

Lighting:
Four 48" (120 cm), 110-watt,
10,000 K VHO fluorescents
(440 watts total)

Filtration:
Two Eheim model 2260
large-capacity canister-style
filters, plumbed through the
aquarium bottom

Substrate:
Fine-grained quartz gravel

Fish:
Sunshine red discus (hybrid),
lemon tetras, cardinal tetras

Water Change:
Once per week, 30 to 40 percent of
tank volume

Water Change:
18-watt UV sterilizer; air pump
controlled by digital timer for lights-
off aeration to benefit discus.

Matching cabinetry integrates the aquarium into the room. The discus's
round shape works well with the many rounded edges of the cabinetry
treatment and dining chairs.

↑

For water changes and maintenance, the aquarium's canopy top is simply raised; it does not have to be removed completely, which is fortunate, as it is quite heavy and requires two people to remove it.

↑

The ozelot sword's ruffled, spotted leaves and the reddish color of the new growth make it a favorite for many discus planted aquariums.

↑

These two discus have paired off and are preparing a branch of driftwood for laying eggs. Although the eggs may hatch, the fry will not survive more than a day or two in an aquarium with so many other fish.

↑

The open foreground provides an excellent area on which food can settle, so the discus may exercise their preferred feeding method— grazing off the bottom.

↑

The hardy and easy-to-grow Amazon sword plant. No trimming is required, just removal of the older outside leaves as they begin to show discoloration, holes, or algae growth.

↑

For daily feeding, the front doors of the canopy top open wide.

| The Inspired Aquarium

Waterfront Home
Live-Planted Aquarium

These homeowners, who wanted an aquarium to harmonize with artwork and interior features, took their time envisioning and planning how the aquarium would affect the many angles and areas of the home from which it would be visible. The result of their attention to detail yielded a functional room-divider aquarium that is both a design focal point for everyday enjoyment and a wonderful conversation piece for their many guests. Dividing the kitchen/casual dining area and the formal dining room and adjacent living room, the aquarium's presence is felt in all the most frequently used areas of the home.

The home is built on the water, the panoramic windows providing lots of natural light to greatly enhance the homeowners' extensive collection of glass artwork and sculpture. Despite their proximity to the ocean, the homeowners were inspired by a nearby bay's grassy inlets and shallows to use a combination of branchy driftwood and greenery that could only be provided by freshwater plants. The aquascape is simple and features the airy impression of the tall, swaying grasses and gold angelfish in contrast to brightly colored, schooling cardinal tetras and clumps of Anubias nana, a short, round-leafed plant that grows well on rocks. Ultrafine, neutral-colored gravel provides a natural sandy floor and is a reminder of substrates that might be found just outside. The overall goal was to keep the primary tones of the aquarium consistent with those of the surrounding space.

Maintenance is kept to a minimum by the use of plants requiring little or no trimming or pruning. The Anubias, which grows beautifully atop the rock structure, does not require any special growing medium or substrate for sustained growth, and the tall grass requires only periodic removal of older blades. This helps the established composition maintain a consistent appearance. As the vegetation grows and matures, it only becomes more lush and lovely.

←
The aquarium serves as the ultimate complement to a space defined by light, water, and glass. It brings a feeling of the surrounding nature into the home.

↓
While this aquarium is close to many windows, it does not receive extended periods of direct sunlight, which helps control algae growth.

Aquarium System and Installation Data

Aquarium Material:
Glass

Aquarium Dimensions:
42" × 36" × 30"
(107 cm × 91 cm × 76 cm)
Support Stand height: 42" (107 cm)

Aquarium Volume:
210 gallons (795 liters)

Lighting:
Four 9-watt, 10,000 K VHO
fluorescents (380 watts total)

Filtration:
One Eheim model 2260 large-
capacity canister-style filter, plumbed
through aquarium bottom

Substrate:
Fluorite (a porous clay growing
media for the planted areas); fine
quartz-based gravel

Plants:
*Cyperus helferi, Vallisneria nana,
Anubias nana*

Fish:
Gold angelfish (hybrid), cardinal
tetra, Siamese algae eater

Water Change:
Once per week, 50 percent of
tank volume

Special Equipment:
Pressurized CO_2 system with 25-watt
UV sterilizer; air pump controlled by
digital timer for lights-off aeration

↓
Matching oak cabinetry and complementary color tones make this
installation truly part of the home. Notice the influence of the painting on
the composition of the aquarium. Outdoor views were also considered
in the design.

↑
The homeowners wanted to be able to see through the aquarium to the bay outside.

↑
Limiting the fish species lends a simple, calming effect to the aquarium. Here, the large, gold angelfish swim gently back and forth, forming ever-changing compositions in an aquatic ballet.

↑
The gold angelfish

↑
The plumbing and system equipment is located underneath the aquarium. Live-planted aquariums do not require much more than simple filtration and a CO_2 supply for sustained growth. Here, a UV sterilizer was incorporated to help keep the water clear at all times.

↑
The tall grass *Cyperus helferi* and the short, round *Anubias nana* are easy to maintain under stable conditions. They create an idyllic underwater scene with little potential for becoming overgrown, like so many other aquatic plant species.

↑
The canopy top is easily removed. The light fixtures and control timers can be stacked or removed to facilitate maintenance. For easier routing of cords, the owners installed a built-in independent power supply.

Chapter 10:
Saltwater Aquarium Case Studies

Suburban Home
Decorative Saltwater Aquarium

This suburban family wanted to add an aquarium to their home as a decorative element and conversation piece. As well, the parents realized the many potential science and educational benefits an aquarium would provide. Knowing little about aquariums—or the variables involved in a custom application such as the freestanding room divider they envisioned—they commissioned a local design, installation, and maintenance company to help. After a short consultation, they were assured that their idea would not only work but also make a beautiful and practical addition to their home. They chose a decorative saltwater aquarium for the amazing fish and heightened style it offers. Several years later, they still enjoy their aquarium and maintain an impressive group of ornamental saltwater fish.

The two-sided aquarium is a classic: bowed glass on the support side and a flat panel on the framed side. The bowed glass adds a touch of style, while the flat side provides the framed appearance of a living canvas that is so desirable.

The aquascape is a fairly traditional cast-mold skeletal coral arrangement with a distinctive round-cupped centerpiece. The goal of the layout is an accommodating setting for the fish, which are the real attraction. To avoid blocking the view between rooms, the aquascape is kept open near the top. This also allows plenty of swimming space for the lionfish and the large puffer, which spend the majority of their swimming time close to the surface (wanting first go at the food!). Some nice barnacle clusters add texture to the bottom and around the bases of the coral. A perfect emperor angelfish is one of the family's prized specimens, and their collection of tangs includes all the hardiest attractive species.

←

A welcome addition to a once-empty wall, this 340-gallon (1,287-liter) decorative saltwater aquarium enlivens the space.

→

A variety of coral shapes makes an appealing composition. The barnacle clusters on the bottom give the layout a natural appearance.

Aquarium System and Installation Data

Aquarium Material:
Glass

Aquarium Dimensions:
72" × 36"× 30"
(183 × 91 × 76 cm)
Support stand height:
42" (107 cm)

Aquarium Volume:
340 gallons (1,287 liters)

Lighting:
Two 165-watt, 10,000 K VHO
fluorescents (330 watts total)

Filtration:
Trickle filter, powered by Iwaki model
30 (flow) magnet-drive pump; one
Eheim model 2260 large-capacity
canister-style filter, plumbed through
aquarium bottom

Substrate: Crushed coral

Fish:
Lionfish, emperor angel, passer
angel, yellow tang, powder-blue
tang, regal blue tang, sailfin tang,
puffer, black damsel

Special Equipment:
¼ horsepower chiller

Water Change: every two
weeks, 40 percent of tank volume

↓
The framed side in the formal living room

↓
A lighted curio area above the aquarium is a
nice touch and gives the installation a feeling
of permanence in the home.

↑
A tidy installation fits all the requisite equipment under the stand. Foam-padded doors and interior for noise reduction are especially important for this aquarium, which is located in the family room.

↑
Two small doors open for daily feeding access and simple maintenance. When necessary, the midsection pulls out to allow full entry into the aquarium for coral removal or other purposes.

←
The fish enjoy the aquascape as well! Most of these specimens have been in the tank since it was established. Diligent maintenance practices and consistent feeding of a variety of foods targeting the needs of each fish have kept them healthy.

↓
A stunning emperor angelfish

Modern Home
Decorative Saltwater Aquarium

A saltwater aquarium with large ornamental fish was part of the architect's original vision for this modern space. With the advantages of a new construction situation, optimal placement was carefully assessed in advance. The idea of placing the aquarium on a corner, maximizing two large viewing windows, was appealing—an opportunity to break with traditional built-in or framed-in installation styles while retaining the clean lines and integrated look. The final plans and ultimate result reveal a museum-quality display that serves focal and peripheral design functions in the multilevel home. The aquarium may be taken in by direct views or more simply perceived from the kitchen, breakfast area, or third-level walkway.

A study in contrasts, the aquascape of this decorative saltwater aquarium features clean, bright coral with dark rocks in a play of light and shadow. The darkened rock and skeletal coral remains convey a sense of the passage of time. The fish, with their potent colors and conceptual forms, play their part in the composition. Forms of nature become forms of art in this well-composed scene. Sharing the space in synchronicity with the art and sculpture, this marine aquarium is in its true element.

A dedicated access and service area was designed behind the aquarium to facilitate the integrated appearance. On-site preparation of replacement water ensures a sufficient volume is changed at each service interval. Because the coral must be cleaned frequently to maintain the desired look, a second set is kept on hand. While one is being cleaned, the other goes straight into the aquarium.

→

Breaking with tradition, a corner placement gives this decorative saltwater aquarium an edge in the space.

Aquarium System and Installation Data

Aquarium Material:
Acrylic

Aquarium Dimensions:
72" × 36" × 48"
(183 ×91 ×122 cm)

Aquarium Volume:
540 gallons (2,043 liters)

Lighting:
Two 250-watt 10,000 K
metal-halide lamps

Filtration:
Trickle filter with biological
media; Precision Marine Systems
bullet protein skimmer

Special Equipment:
¼-horsepower chiller

Fish:
Lionfish, gold puffer, sailfin tangs,
clown trigger, Niger trigger, black and
white *Heniochus*, diamond *Anthias*

Water Change:
Every two weeks, 40 percent of
tank volume

Like a work of modern sculpture, the decorative saltwater aquarium
is most at home in a modern interior. Note the subtle use of color
in the vases, pillows, and artwork that tie the space together with
the aquarium.

Two 250-watt metal-halide light fixtures illuminate the display. Each is on a separate digital timer so neither fixture is always on, or on for too long. Much of the time, only one fixture is used, which helps control algae growth. The second fixture is great for special viewing occasions.

Behind the scenes, an exceptional rear-access room was designed for system equipment, service access, frozen fish food storage, and water purification and mixing. Behind the door are storage cabinets and a dedicated sink.

This full aquarium shot gives a sense of the dimensions of this impressive display. The height makes some aspects of maintenance difficult, such as reaching the bottom or front of the layout. If the front areas must be reached, long-handled grabber tongs are used.

What a face! The golden puffer exemplifies the otherworldly characteristics of so many marine fish.

Placement of the aquarium in the corner ensures its presence is felt from three levels of the home. Acrylic was the material of choice to accommodate the 48" (122 cm) height as well as to soften the corner edge.

Home Theater Live
Coral Reef Aquarium

This home theater installation benefited from being designed by the homeowner, who just happens to be a designer herself. Rini Wu Ziegler of Ziegler Design has a longstanding passion for aquariums and had them in previous homes. This time around, on a complete remodel of an existing residence, she wanted to push the limits of aquarium design by working with the dimensions of the tank itself. She envisioned an aquarium that was like a long sliver across the wall opposite the drop-down LCD projection screen. The final design yielded an incredible aquarium that is 96" (244 cm) long and only 14" (36 cm) tall.

A live coral reef style proved a perfect match for the decidedly modern aesthetics of the space. High-tech, abstract, and vivid, the live coral reef style fulfills the need for brightness to compensate for the sliver presentation. At such a short height, if the aquarium were too subdued, its impact would be lost. Additionally, live corals benefit from the intense light possible at such shallow depths.

Because the aquarium is situated in a home theater, system noise was a concern. The pumps and other equipment generate noise levels that may be fine for larger spaces or areas with sufficient background noise to counter them, but in a small theater room, with the viewers sitting close to the aquarium, it would certainly be a problem. The inventive solution here was to place the system components in a protected housing outdoors.

The aquascape is kept simple and straightforward by stretching the live rock structure down the middle of the aquarium. Hardy coral species that tolerate intense light were selected, while special attention was also paid to the light fixtures. The pendant-style metal halides raise and lower with ease, so they can be adjusted to just the right height above the aquarium—a good example of the type of system design planning essential to the successful completion of such a uniquely proportioned aquarium.

←

A one-of-a-kind "silver" style live-coral reef aquarium is the definitive touch to a home theater room. Because the room is fairly small, design elements were chosen carefully, especially the aquarium itself, which pairs well with the modern furniture and light fixture.

Aquarium System and Installation Data

Aquarium Material:
Glass

Aquarium Dimensions:
96" × 14" × 14"
(244 cm × 36 cm × 36 cm)
Support stand height: 36" (90 cm)

Aquarium Volume:
125 gallons (473 liters)

Lighting:
Three 250-watt, 14,000 K
HQI halogens, pendant type

Filtration:
Acrylic sump with particulate sponge
(no biological media) powered by
Iwaki model 55 tmagnet-drive pump;
Precision Marine Systems bullet
protein skimmer

Invertebrates:
Candy corals (*Colastrea*), finger
leather coral, umbrella leather,
yellow devil's hand leather,
mushroom rocks, open brain
corals (red and green), green star
polyps, colt corals, red button coral,
Acropora sp., bird's nest coral,
slipper tongue corals, cup corals,
meat corals, colonial polyps, feather-
duster tubeworms, Maxima clam,
Squamosa clam, Crocea clam, Gigas
clam

Fish:
Ocellaris clownfish, yellow tang,
regal blue tang, green chromis,
flame hawkfish, six-line wrasse

Water Change:
Once per week, 15 percent of tank
volume

Special Equipment:
¼ horsepower chiller

←
Like the midday Sun over a tide pool,
pendant-style HQI halogen fixtures illuminate
the shallows of this remarkable aquarium.

↓
Corals, clams, and feather-duster worms
take in the ample light and strong current.

↑
Although the aquarium is shallow, the well-executed layout provides dramatic close-up views. A feeling of depth is evident despite the limited width.

↑
An effective aquascape in tricky dimensions. Corals of just the right size were needed to achieve a balanced, linear composition.

←
An outdoor filtration house works perfectly with the simple inflow and outflow design.

Bed and Bath Live Coral Reef Aquarium

As someone who had always dreamed of having a beautiful marine aquarium, it was beyond this homeowner's fondest hopes to have a single aquarium that functioned like two. He had always imagined it in the living room, but when the opportunity arose during the building of a custom home to incorporate an aquarium into the master bedroom and bath, the idea seemed perfect. The result was beyond expectation; the live coral reef aquarium transformed the space into a glorious retreat and can be enjoyed while relaxing in the tub or settling into the sheets.

The design of this aquarium makes no particular attempt to harmonize with the space but works nonetheless. Any style could have worked in these rooms; the reef aquarium happened to be the homeowner's first choice.

On the bedroom side, the aquarium assumes a framed, built-in look. However, instead of the traditional approach of creating a freestanding installation opposite the framed-in side, the bathroom side of the aquarium also has a built-in appearance. Positioned above a gas fireplace, it is protected from fireplace heat by heat-shield material and a customized ventilation system.

The layout of the live rock structure is a classic U-shape—perfect for privacy between the two rooms while maintaining their connection through the midsection of the composition. An archway was skillfully incorporated to allow fish to move freely between the two sides. The concealed overflow box leaves the aquarium looking natural and unencumbered. System components were cleverly placed under the sink next to the aquarium.

To ensure good overall sustainability, the aquarium was stocked with the hardiest corals, invertebrates, and reef fishes. Large mushroom corals form the focal points on the bedroom side, with soft corals and stony corals defining the bathroom side.

←
A two-sided live coral reef aquarium in a bedroom is installed over a fireplace. The classic framed-in design allows the aquarium to function like a living canvas.

Aquarium System and Installation Data

Aquarium Material:
Glass

Aquarium Dimensions:
48" × 24"× 30"
(122 cm × 61 cm × 76 cm)
Support stand height: 42" (107 cm)

Aquarium Volume:
150 gallons (568 liters)

Lighting:
Two 250-watt, 14,000 K metal-halide lamps with two 110-watt, actinic 03 VHO fluorescents (720 watts total)

Filtration:
Acrylic sump with particulate sponge (no biological media) powered by Iwaki model 55 magnet-drive pump; Precision Marine Systems bullet protein skimmer

Invertebrates:
Assorted frogspawn corals, torch corals, mushroom rocks, colt corals, green star polyps, yellow polyps, colonial polyps, leather corals, cup corals, giant cup mushroom corals, meat coral (*Lobophyllia*), button coral, purple whip gorgonian coral, hammer corals, candy corals, red flower pot coral (*Gonipora*), feather-duster tubeworms, cleaner shrimps

Fish:
Powder-blue tang, yellow tang, sailfin tang, *Anthias* sp., false percula clownfish, yellow choris wrasse, neon damsel, green chromis, lightning wrasse

Water Change:
Every two weeks, 30 percent of tank volume

←
The design and build-out on the bathroom side takes on a different look from the bedroom side; the impression is of two different aquariums altogether.

↑
The aquascape allows just enough view between the two spaces. The bridge linking the two main structures is a nice touch.

↑
The angle of the slope is both visually pleasing and functional. The corals can be worked into place easily and remain stable.

→
Who would think the filtration system was plumbed in underneath the sink? High marks are earned here for superb design forethought! The chiller is positioned outside the house for maximum ventilation.

↓
No access issues here—the big doors swing open wide and allow generous access to both sides of the aquarium.

↘
Good ventilation is needed above the aquarium to eliminate the heat generated by the light fixtures. A simple fan does the job, although planning for the hole was required in the design phase.

Urban High-Rise Condominium Live Coral Reef Aquarium

The inclusion of a live coral reef aquarium in this luxury high-rise condominium was suggested by the lead architect commissioned to renovate the space. The clients, avid art lovers and collectors, were excited about the prospect of an aquarium that would hold up among their treasured pieces and fabulous décor. Their goal was a freestanding work of living sculpture; the nature component was a bonus. In an urban environment without much in the way of natural surroundings, the live coral reef aquarium provides the right balance of nature and art. Design forethought and planning were essential to determining the aquarium's ideal placement—an island-style installation.

The aquarium is a focal point of the first-floor space. Because attention was paid to determining angles of view, the aquarium is positioned so it can be seen from the entryway, both formal and informal dining areas, and the living room.

The well-composed aquascape assumes a strong downward slope from the overflow box and leaves an open area at one end of the aquarium. This composition style is excellent for an installation that requires an overflow box because it conceals the box on the high side while allowing for openness on the low side. The sloping layout also provides a space-dividing effect, adding to the function of the aquarium as a whole in the space.

The corals and other marine life in the aquarium heighten the effectiveness of the aquarium as an art piece. Their colors and textures play well against patterns present in the paintings, sculpture, and art glass.

Maintenance is simple, thanks to plenty of planning time during the initial renovation phase. Because reef aquariums do not have much latitude in terms of maintenance requirements, every possible routine service convenience was built into an innovative service closet located just a few feet away. The result is an aquarium without compromise.

←

The abstract and strangely beautiful forms of the ocean come together in the live coral reef aquarium. This one seems right at home near a work by Joan Miró, the great twentieth-century Spanish abstractionist.

→

An inspired aquarium in an inspired space. No other style would have carried the same impact as the live coral reef aquarium in this setting.

Aquarium System and Installation Data

Aquarium Material:
Glass

Aquarium Dimensions:
72" × 36" × 36"
(183 cm × 91 cm × 91 cm)
Support stand height: 42" (107 cm)

Aquarium Volume:
400 gallons (1,514 liters)

Lighting:
Three 400-watt, 14,000 K metal
halide lamps with two 165-watt,
actinic 03 VHO fluorescents (1,530
watts total)

Filtration:
Acrylic sump with particulate sponge
(no biological media) powered by a
Sequence Dart main pump; Precision
Marine Systems bullet protein
skimmer

Invertebrates:
Assorted hammer corals, frogspawn
corals, cup corals, green star polyps,
galaxial star corals, mushroom
corals, button coral, umbrella leather
corals, Caribbean gorgonian corals
(purple whip and knobby), torch
corals, open brain corals, colonial
polyps, colt (*Cludellia*) corals, bubble
corals, elegance coral, branching
flowerpot coral (*Goniopora*), giant
cup mushrooms, meat coral
(*Lobophyllia*), finger leather coral,

yellow polyps, green Maxima clam,
Derasa clam

Fish:
Christmas wrasse, yellow tang, blue
(hippo) tang, purple tang, powder-
blue tang, *Anthias* sp., false percula
clownfish, green chromis damsel,
long-nosed hawkfish, scissortail
goby, pajama cardinalfish

Special Equipment:
¼-horsepower chiller

Water Change:
Every two weeks, 30 percent of tank
volume (water added weekly
for evaporation)

↓
An island-style installation means this aquarium
is omnipresent in the seamless floor plan.

↓
A beautiful installation—compact and
efficient

↓
Foam insulation on cabinet doors lowers
noise from the main pump and chiller
(bottom).

↑
 This aquarium is still fairly new (about six months old when photographed), so many of the corals have yet to reach their full potential. Desirable coralline algae are just starting to form on the live rock structure.

↑
A charming, long-nosed hawkfish perches beneath the coral.

↑
An offering of varied coral species is a feast for the eyes.

↑
A dynamic view from the entryway at dusk

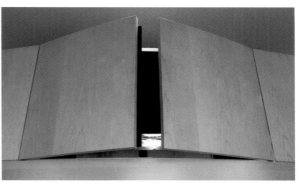

↑
Routine access to the aquarium is through doors located on both sides of the canopy top.

↑
An ingenious closet for on-site saltwater preparation is located close to the aquarium.

↑
The door snaps open to reveal the mixing vat and reverse osmosis purification system. The design ensures that a consistent supply of prepared water is always at hand. The high-rise location makes transporting enough saltwater for a substantial water change up to the aquarium impractical.

Resources

Aquarium Websites by Subject

Websites come and go, however, and some websites may no longer exist or have changed URLs.

Installation and Maintenance Companies

Due to the regional nature of custom aquarium design, installation, and maintenance firms, it is impossible to recommend many specifically. Research companies in your area to find one suited to your desired project or need.

Aquariclean, Inc. (Chicago, USA)
773.774.3474
www.aquariclean.com

Aquarium Design Group (Houston, USA)
713.622.6467
www.aquariumdesigngroup.com

Aquarium Network (New York, USA)
515.798.4727
www.aquariumnetwork.net

Blue Zoo Aquatics (Los Angeles, USA)
310.952.0160
www.bluezooaquatics.com

House of Fins (Greenwich, Connecticut, USA)
203.661.8131
www.houseoffins.com

Living Art Aquatic Design, Inc. (Los Angeles, USA)
310.234.3333
www.aquatic2000.com

Living Color Enterprises, Inc. (Ft. Lauderdale, Florida, USA)
800.878.9511
www.livingcolor.com

Aquarium Products

The following online retailers offer a variety of quality aquarium products, information, and links to other useful websites.

Aqua Direct (USA)
www.aquadirect.com

Aqua Essentials (UK)
www.aquaessentials.co.uk

Abissi (Italy)
www.abissi.com

Big-Al's (Canada/USA)
www.bigalsonline.com

Marine Depot (USA)
www.marinedepot.com

Reef Splendor (USA)
www.reefsplendor.com

SeaMe (Netherlands)
www.seame.com

Vivid Aquariums (USA)
www.vividaquariums.com

Aquarium Product Manufacturers

Some of the following manufacturers are wholesale-only, but may offer catalogs, references, or other useful information.

Aqua Design Amano (Japan)
www.adana.co.jp
Nature-style (live-planted) aquarium goods, including aquariums, stands, filters, specialized substrates for growing aquatic plants, fertilizers, and unique glassware.

Aquatic Nature (Europe)
www.aquatic-nature.com
Products including gravels and substrates, equipment, specialized foods, and more for fresh and saltwater aquariums.

CaribSea, Inc. (USA)
www.carib-sea.com
Manufactures a wide variety of specialized substrates for freshwater and saltwater aquariums.

Coralife (USA)
www.esuweb.com
Manufactures a complete line of aquarium light fixtures and bulbs, aquarium salt, and water conditioners.

Dennerle (Europe)
www.dennerle.de
Products for live-planted aquariums.

Eheim (Germany)
www.eheim.com
Manufactures canister-style aquarium filters, filter media, aquariums, and more.

Kent Marine (USA)
www.kentmarine.com
Manufactures a complete line of fresh and saltwater aquarium supplements, water conditioners, maintenance tools, foods, and more.

Oceanic Systems, Inc. (USA)
www.oceanicsystems.com
Manufactures high-quality glass aquariums—both production and custom.

Precision Marine Systems (USA)
www.precisionmarine.com
Manufactures protein skimmers, sumps, trickle filters, and more.

SeaChem Laboratories (USA)
www.seachem.com
Freshwater and saltwater products, including water conditioners, buffers, filtration media, medications, test kits, and gravels.

Aquatic Plants

Aqua Botanic (USA)
www.aquabotanic.com

Arizona Aquatic Gardens (USA)
www.a-zgardens.com

Freshwater Aquarium Plants (USA)
www.freshwateraquariumplants.com

Tropica (Denmark)
www.tropica.com

Corals

The following suppliers offer live corals. High-quality local retail shops are also a good source of live corals.

frags.org (USA)
www.frags.org

Reefer Madness (USA)
www.reefermadness.us

Online Forums

Acqua Portal Italy
www.acquaportal.it

Aquarium Pros
www.aquariumpros.com

Aquatic-Photography Forum
www.aquatic-photography.com

Aquatic Plant Central
www.aquaticplantcentral.com

Info Pez (Spain)
www.infopez.com

The Planted Tank
www.plantedtank.net

Ultimate Reef.com
www.ultimatereef.net

Clubs and Associations

Almost every major city has an aquarium society or club of some kind. Some are style-specific (for example, live-planted aquarium, reef aquarium, cichlids), while others are general.

American Cichlid Association
www.cichlid.org

Aquatic Gardeners Association
www.aquatic-gardeners.org

Federation of American Aquarium Societies
www.gcca.net/faas/

Marine Aquarium Societies of North America
www.masna.org

The Angelfish Society
www.theangelfishsociety.org

Informational Websites

Aquarium Hobbyist
www.aquariumhobbyist.com
Online community of freshwater, marine, and reef hobbyists

Auqgrass (China)
www.auqgrass.com
Information on aquatic plants

Barr Report
www.barrreport.com
Special focus on the science of live-planted aquariums

Greenstouch
www.greenstouch.com
Aquatic plants, aquarium photography

The Krib
www.thekrib.com
Tropical fish information, great links

Oliver Knott the Aqua Creator (Germany)
www.pbase.com/plantella
Site for one of Europe's foremost aquascape designers

reefs.org
www.reefs.org
Lots of information, discussion, and links pertaining to reef aquariums

Wet Web Media
www.wetwebmedia.com
Aquariums, fish, and aquatic information

Magazines

Aqua Journal (Japanese publication)
(Aqua Design Amano Co. Ltd.)
www.adana.co.jp

Aqua Planta/Reef Art (Italian publication)
(AquaEdi)
www.aquaedi.info

Aqua Plaisir (French publication)
(Aquamedia)
www.aquaplaisir.com

Hydra (Italian publication)
(Sixth Continent Publishers)
www.spaziohydra.com

Practical Fishkeeping Magazine (UK)
(Emap) www.practicalfishkeeping.co.uk

The Aquatic Gardener (USA)
(The Aquatic Gardeners Association)
www.aquatic-gardeners.org

Tropical Fish Hobbyist (USA)
(T.F.H. Publications, Inc.)
www.tfhmagazine.com

Tropical World (UK)
www.tropicalworldmagazine.com

Books

Aquarium Atlas
by Hans A. Baensch & Dr. George W. Fischer
(Mergus/Microcosm Ltd.)

Aquarium Plants
by Christel Kasselmann (Krieger Publishing Company)

A Pocket Expert Guide: Marine Invertebrates
by Ronald L. Shimek (T.F.H Publications)

A Pocket Expert Guide: Marine Fishes
by Scott W. Michael (T.F.H. Publications)

Nature Aquarium World, Vol. 1, 2, & 3
by Takashi Amano (T.F.H. Publications)

The Conscientious Marine Aquarist
by Robert M. Fenner (T.F.H. Publications)

The Natural Aquarium
by Satoshi Yoshino & Doshin Kobayashi (T.F.H. Publications)

Index

Acknowledgments

A very special thanks to the staff at Aquarium Design Group: Doug Petranoff, Holt Harlan, Markus Tollefson, Travis and Lee Clifton, Scott Wisneski, Shannon and Tara Rice, Ryan Carrico, Bryant Logan, Chris Nguyen, and Eric Senske.

A huge thanks to our father, Dr. Andy Senske, for keeping the dream alive, and to our families for their tireless support throughout this project, especially Dani, Eli, and Nora.

An enormous debt of gratitude is due to Mr. Takashi Amano for his boundless inspiration, vision, and advancement of the aquarium arts. His spirit and wisdom are with us always.

Thanks also to our editor, Pat Price, and photography coordinator, Betsy Gammons, for their brilliance and patience.

About the Authors

Brothers Jeff and Mike Senske are the founders of Aquarium Design Group, a progressive, full-service aquarium design and installation firm. Avid hobbyists their entire lives, they have worked in virtually every aspect of the aquarium industry. In their work, they seek always to elevate the art of aquarium keeping with a strong penchant for design innovation and aquascapes that eschew the traditional notions of aquarium design. Both have been recognized internationally for their design work and aquarium photography, which has been featured in many industry publications and websites. The Senske brothers' passion for the aquarium arts and devotion to the establishment of high industry standards keep them at the forefront of one of the world's most enduring and popular hobbies.